97 Things Every Data Engineer Should Know

Collective Wisdom from the Experts

Tobias Macey

Beijing · Boston · Farnham · Sebastopol · Tokyo

97 Things Every Data Engineer Should Know

by Tobias Macey

Copyright © 2021 O'Reilly Media, Inc. All rights reserved.

Published by O'Reilly Media, Inc., 1005 Gravenstein Highway North, Sebastopol, CA 95472.

O'Reilly books may be purchased for educational, business, or sales promotional use. Online editions are also available for most titles (*http://oreilly.com*). For more information, contact our corporate/institutional sales department: 800-998-9938 or *corporate@oreilly.com*.

Acquisitions Editor: Jessica Haberman
Developmental Editor: Jill Leonard
Production Editor: Beth Kelly
Copyeditor: Sharon Wilkey
Proofreader: Rachel Head

Indexer: WordCo Indexing Services, Inc.
Interior Designer: Monica Kamsvaag
Cover Designer: Randy Comer
Illustrator: Kate Dullea

June 2021:   First Edition

Revision History for the First Edition
2021-06-11:   First Release

See *http://oreilly.com/catalog/errata.csp?isbn=9781492062417* for release details.

978-1-492-06241-7

[LSI]

Table of Contents

Preface

Data engineering as a distinct role is relatively new, but the responsibilities have existed for decades. Broadly speaking, a data engineer makes data available for use in analytics, machine learning, business intelligence, etc. The introduction of big data technologies, data science, distributed computing, and the cloud have all contributed to making the work of the data engineer more necessary, more complex, and (paradoxically) more possible. It is an impossible task to write a single book that encompasses everything that you will need to know to be effective as a data engineer, but there are still a number of core principles that will help you in your journey.

This book is a collection of advice from a wide range of individuals who have learned valuable lessons about working with data the hard way. To save you the work of making their same mistakes, we have collected their advice to give you a set of building blocks that can be used to lay your own foundation for a successful career in data engineering.

In these pages you will find career tips for working in data teams, engineering advice for how to think about your tools, and fundamental principles of distributed systems. There are many paths into data engineering, and no two people will use the same set of tools, but we hope that you will find the inspiration that will guide you on your journey. So regardless of whether this is your first step on the road, or you have been walking it for years we wish you the best of luck in your adventures.

O'Reilly Online Learning

 For more than 40 years, *O'Reilly Media* has provided technology and business training, knowledge, and insight to help companies succeed.

Our unique network of experts and innovators share their knowledge and expertise through books, articles, and our online learning platform. O'Reilly's online learning platform gives you on-demand access to live training courses, in-depth learning paths, interactive coding environments, and a vast collection of text and video from O'Reilly and 200+ other publishers. For more information, visit *http://oreilly.com*.

How to Contact Us

Please address comments and questions about this book to the publisher:

O'Reilly Media, Inc.
1005 Gravenstein Highway North
Sebastopol, CA 95472
800-998-9938 (in the United States or Canada)
707-829-0515 (international or local)
707-829-0104 (fax)

We have a web page for this book, where we list errata, examples, and any additional information. You can access this page at *https://oreil.ly/97-things-data-eng*.

Email *bookquestions@oreilly.com* to comment or ask technical questions about this book.

Visit *http://oreilly.com* for news and information about our books and courses.

Find us on Facebook: *http://facebook.com/oreilly*

Follow us on Twitter: *http://twitter.com/oreillymedia*

Watch us on YouTube: *http://youtube.com/oreillymedia*

Acknowledgments

I would like to thank my wife for her help and support while I worked on this book, the numerous contributors for sharing their time and expertise, and the O'Reilly team for all of their hard work to make this book a reality.

A (Book) Case for Eventual Consistency

Denise Koessler Gosnell, PhD

Consider the life of owning a bookstore.[1] At some point, you will want to set up a system that maintains an inventory of all the books in your store.

In the store's early days, you selected a system that was designed for about 1,000 books at one location. This system updates a book's record during a customer's checkout. When a customer approaches the counter to buy a book, your inventory system does the following:

1. Checks your ledgers for inventory details
2. Records the new purchase
3. Updates all the records
4. Returns a receipt to the customer

The receipt confirms both the customer's purchase and that your inventory system is up-to-date. This type of inventory system requires all of your transactions to have strong consistency. In this sense, *strong consistency* refers to all accesses to the store's inventory being processed sequentially and read from the same state in your store's inventory system.

Well, good news, store owner! The book business is booming, and you are opening multiple stores to address your growing customer base. In this world, how do you maintain your company's inventory across multiple stores?

Maybe you consider rearchitecting your current system. You decide to have one master register in your first store. Then, all of your other stores will have a new register that connects to the master.

---

1 Denise Gosnell would like to thank David Bechberger (*https://oreil.ly/BnxMV*) for his contributions to this chapter.

This new system works great...until you lose power to your master register. Now all of the customers at all of your stores are blocked from making a single purchase. Your lines are long and stagnant.

Are you going to let your customers walk away frustrated when your queue takes too long to process? To resolve this, maybe you decide that validating and updating your store's inventory can be done in a different way.

Maybe this time you consider updating your ledgers on a daily basis. In this new system, at nightly close, you update the inventory of your books by counting all of them in each store and validating that each title you expect is on your shelves. Each night, your stores' shelves pass their tests, and you can go home resting assured that your books are balanced.

This second type of inventory system plans for all of your transactions to have *eventual consistency*. Each access to your store's inventory is processed in parallel and logs an update to your book's inventory system. *Eventually*, all accesses about a particular book will return the last updated value.

And what happens if a customer goes to look for a title that isn't on your shelves? Well, you can address it then.

Addressing inconsistencies when they are found is like *read repair* in a distributed system. Only when you find an inconsistency do you kick off the heavier process to update state across all of your ledgers. During this process, you can inspect your sales logs to see whether the records are up-to-date. The result of these multiple inspections of state is to ensure that your records are up-to-date and consistent.

Is this process good enough for you? For systems that have to trade high-volume processing for state consistency, yes.

Swapping to an eventually consistent system with read repair to address inconsistencies will keep your customers from the peril of long lines at the register. And it will keep your architects feeling less stress about protecting the availability of your master register's database.

Loosely speaking, the two approaches to keeping inventory in your store represent two schools of thought. They describe two different architectures: one that is *strongly consistent* (addressing scale with client/server–style architectures) and another that is *eventually consistent* (handling high-volume transactions and resolving stateful inconsistencies when they are found).

So for the system you are designing, what school of thought do you want to plan with?

A/B and How to Be

Sonia Mehta

At its core, *A/B testing* is a method of comparing two versions of something, to see which one performs better. A very simple example of this is adjusting the location of an ecommerce site's shopping cart image from the top right to the bottom right. Perhaps some team members believe moving it to the bottom will lead to fewer abandoned carts. Depending on the size and nature of the experiment, data engineering may be involved with everything from the instrumentation and tracking to the analysis.

Related to this topic, it's important to know that third-party tools exist to help set up backend tracking for experiments. Whether a third-party tool or an in-house solution is used, it's critical to validate the results and feel comfortable about the experiment logging.

In validating experiment metrics, nuances will always need further investigating. The list can be quite long, but areas that can allow you to quickly detect an issue include the following:

Sample sizes
> If the experiment is a 50/50 split, the sample sizes should be very close to one another. If the experiment is another split, validate the sample size against the expected weight.

Start and stop dates (with any ramp-up weights)
> The experiment may have been slowly rolled out in a ladder, from 1%, 5%, 10%, etc., to avoid a potentially large adverse impact. The experiment may have also had a bug (in design, randomization, etc.) or been run during a holiday period, and data from those periods may need to be excluded or evaluated separately.

User in both groups
> If a user was erroneously fed both the control and the experiment, that user will need to be excluded from the experiment. (If this is a widespread problem, the experiment may have to be redone.)

Context-specific restrictions

Depending on the experiment, there may also be specific restrictions on users that receive the experiment. For example, an airline may provide the same experience to all users under the same booking ID. This may create moments of imbalance in sample sizes for an experiment, but should self-resolve.

When changes are made to the experimentation backend process, you should consider running an *A/A test*. This kind of test serves the same experience to all users. Its purpose is to ensure that the instrumentation and logging are collecting correctly. When an experiment is live, discerning whether a tracking error is present can be difficult, because it can get masked by the experiment results themselves. Conversely, the error could be easy to detect, but if it's detected after an experiment has gone live, the experiment will likely need to be paused to correct for the issue and then reinitiated, losing valuable time.

Expect most experiments to fail. Netflix considers 90% of what it tries to be wrong.[1] Knowing this, expect a lot of questions! Expect questions around the accuracy of the instrumentation and logging. When you see a dramatic improvement with an experiment, be skeptical. You may want to reevaluate the results and analyze again on the full rollout.

Lastly, don't be hard on yourself! Experimentation is complex, and as you continue to work in the field, you'll learn more and be able to better triage questions.

---

1 See *Do It Wrong Quickly: How the Web Changes the Old Marketing Rules* by Mike Moran (IBM Press).

About the Storage Layer

Julien Le Dem

The main purpose of abstractions in software is to hide complexity. Just as we prove mathematical theorems by using other theorems that have previously been proven, we build software on top of abstraction layers without needing to know exactly how they are implemented. We may understand them; we just don't need to have every detail in mind when we use them, freeing up our thoughts to concentrate on what we're trying to achieve.

That said, it is useful (but not necessary) to actually go through these details at least once. Understanding assembly language or compilers makes us better programmers, even if we don't fiddle with them on a day-to-day basis. The same is true of the storage layer of a database or any data-processing framework.

This *storage layer* is what provides the familiar two-dimensional table abstraction on top of a linear persistence layer. For example, while writing SQL, we focus on defining constraints that define a result (joins, filters, etc.) without needing to know the data format or layout. The optimizer will figure out an efficient way to produce the correct result.

A naive query engine would load the data in memory and then apply filters and other expressions. Naturally, we want to avoid loading anything that will be discarded as part of query processing. This saves I/O cost as well as CPU cost by avoiding the subsequent deserialization. We also want to reduce the data footprint, so the data costs less to store and is faster to retrieve. A combination of encodings and compression provides a trade-off between decreasing I/O cost and increasing CPU cost. The throughput of the storage will dictate how much CPU to use, and cheap decoding techniques are paramount.

Those implementation details are usually hidden behind what is commonly known as *pushdowns*. These push query operations into the storage layer to minimize the cost of loading the data. They come in a few flavors.

First, a *projection pushdown* consists of reading only the columns requested. Second, a *predicate pushdown* consists of avoiding deserializing rows that are going to be discarded by a filter. Lastly, partial aggregations and function/expression evaluation can be pushed down to avoid materializing intermediary data. They define our abstraction: What columns do you need? How do you filter the rows? What expression do you apply to them?

Various storage characteristics will impact the performance of pushdowns. Columnar layouts (for example, in Apache Parquet) enable projection pushdowns and better encodings and compression. Statistics (like minimum and maximum values) at different levels of granularity enable predicate pushdowns. For example, if the max value for a row group is smaller than any value that can match a filter, we can skip reading and deserializing it entirely. Sorting and partitioning data—possibly on different columns (as enabled by Apache Iceberg)—will make both compression and predicate pushdowns more efficient, since statistics will more precisely narrow the data to read.

Analytics as the Secret Glue for Microservice Architectures

Elias Nema

Recently, we've seen a major shift toward microservice architectures. Driven by the industry's most successful companies, this allowed teams to have fewer dependencies, move faster, and scale more easily. But, of course, it also introduced challenges. Most are related to the architecture's distributed nature and the increased cost of communication.

Lots of progress has been made to overcome these challenges, mostly in the areas of system observability and operations. The journey itself is treated as a technical problem to solve. Analytics is often overlooked as something not having a direct relation to the system design. However, the heterogeneous nature of microservices makes a perfect case for data analysis.

That's how data warehouses were born, after all—as *central repositories of integrated data from one or more disparate sources.* In a distributed setup, the role of the company-wide analytical platform can be immense. Let's look at an example.

Imagine that your team releases a feature. You run an experiment and notice that the feature drives up your team's target key performance indicator (KPI). That's great. Should you roll it out for the entire user base? Sure, roll out, celebrate, and go home. What if, however, at the same time, another KPI for a different team goes down? This might happen when you cannibalize a channel or introduce major behavior changes on a platform. Would you want to release this feature now?

Of course, there is no correct answer to this. Nor is there a template of any kind. Making a decision requires careful planning of the experiment, cross-team alignment, and a willingness to make small dips where needed so the whole system moves optimally, not the single component. Having data provides a common ground for these decisions, allows companies to make an educated guess, and provides the ability to estimate the impact. Without data, teams might fall into a vicious cycle of pulling in different directions, resulting in a lot of movement with no progress.

So which metrics should you think of when starting a new project or planning an experiment? Consider the following:

Company's high-level metrics
These are the hardest to move, and rarely will be shifted by a single experiment or feature. They are more likely to be altered by the compound effect of many iterations.

Team's metrics
You do want to drive up your team metrics, but the important factor here is to look at them in the context of being a part of a system.

More-granular experiments or project-related metrics
These usually come to mind when designing a feature. They should be as detailed as possible so you can measure the direct and isolated impact.

There might be more metrics, depending on the project. Only by looking through various levels of detail will you be able to make data-conscious decisions and have the grounds for communicating them.

That's why, when stepping onto the path of microservices, a company-wide analytical and experimentation culture should be among the prerequisites, not an afterthought. A rich analytical platform can become the glue that connects separate elements of a system. It also allows you to orchestrate loosely coupled components to sway in the same direction.

Automate Your Infrastructure

Christiano Anderson

One of the roles of data engineers is to deploy data pipelines by using a cloud service provider like Amazon Web Services (AWS), Google Cloud Platform (GCP), Microsoft Azure, or others. We can easily use the web console to link components together and provide a full data pipeline.

Considering AWS as an example, we may want to use API Gateway as our representational state transfer (REST) interface to perform data ingestion, a few Lambda functions to validate the ingestion, Kinesis Data Streams to provide a real-time analysis, Kinesis Data Firehose to deliver the data, and Simple Storage Service (S3) as a persistence layer. We may also want to use Athena as a visualization layer.

With this example, we have to deal with about six components. Each component may require additional setup. Finally, we have to deal with a lot of identity and access management (IAM) roles to handle permissions and access-control lists (ACLs). OK, we can do everything by clicking the console and linking all the components together; this is the fastest way to create your infrastructure if you just need one simple ingestion pipeline.

But if you have to set everything up by hand again, and again, and again, it will require a lot of extra time and provide more opportunities to make mistakes, or even open a security breach. That is why data engineers must learn how to automate their code. Here are some guidelines:

Never use the web console
> Choose an infrastructure-as-code tool to do this (for example, Terraform or AWS CloudFormation).

Make it modular
> For example, use one module to deploy your API gateway, another module to deploy Kinesis, an additional module to manage IAM roles, and so forth. Most tools allow you to reuse your code in various components

(for example, sharing IAM policies to write only once and use everywhere).

Use a version-control system to manage your code
This is helpful if you work on a team; you can enable a pull-request option to check the code before applying it to the master branch.

Test the code before applying the changes
Terraform, for example, shows you all the changes in your infrastructure before applying them. This allows you to avoid breaking your infrastructure.

Use a continuous integration/continuous delivery (CI/CD) pipeline
You can automate everything and make your job much easier by using a CI/CD pipeline.

If you have never used this approach before, dedicate some time to studying Terraform or CloudFormation, and then write all your infrastructure as code. The time and effort required will be worthwhile: you will have full control of your infrastructure, and it will enable you to deploy a brand-new data pipeline in minutes, by just executing your infrastructure code.

Automate Your Pipeline Tests

Tom White

By sticking to the following guidelines when building data pipelines, and treating data engineering like software engineering, you can write well-factored, reliable, and robust pipelines.

Build an End-to-End Test of the Whole Pipeline

Don't put any effort into what the pipeline does at this stage. Focus on infrastructure: how to provide known input, do a simple transform, and test that the output is as expected. Use a regular unit-testing framework like JUnit or pytest.

Use a Small Amount of Representative Data

It should be small enough that the test can run in a few minutes at most. Ideally, this data is from your real (production) system (but make sure it is anonymized).

Prefer Textual Data Formats over Binary

Data files should be diff-able, so you can quickly see what's happening when a test fails. You can check the input and expected outputs into version control and track changes over time.

If the pipeline accepts or produces only binary formats, consider adding support for text in the pipeline itself, or do the necessary conversion in the test.

Ensure That Tests Can Be Run Locally

Running tests locally makes debugging test failures as easy as possible. Use in-process versions of the systems you are using, like Apache Spark's local mode or Apache HBase's minicluster, to provide a self-contained local environment.

Minimize use of cloud services in tests. They can provide a uniform environment but may add friction in terms of provisioning time, debuggability, and access (e.g., users have to provide their own credentials for open source projects). Run the tests under CI too, of course.

Make Tests Deterministic

Sometimes the order of output records doesn't matter in your application. For testing, however, you may want an extra step to sort by a field to make the output stable.

Some algorithms use randomness—for example, a clustering algorithm to choose candidate neighbors. Setting a seed is standard practice, but may not help in a distributed setting where workers perform operations in a nondeterministic order. In this case, consider running that part of the test pipeline with a single worker, or seeding per data partition.

Avoid having variable time fields be a part of the output. This should be possible by providing fixed input; otherwise, consider mocking out time, or post-processing the output to strip out time fields. If all else fails, match outputs by a similarity measure rather than strict equality.

Make It Easy to Add More Tests

Parameterize by input file so you can run the same test on multiple inputs. Consider adding a switch that allows the test to record the output for a new edge case input, so you can eyeball it for correctness and add it as expected output.

Be Intentional About the Batching Model in Your Data Pipelines

Raghotham Murthy

If you are ingesting data records in batches and building batch data pipelines, you will need to choose how to create the batches over a period of time. Batches can be based on the `data_timestamp` or the `arrival_timestamp` of the record. The `data_timestamp` is the last updated timestamp included in the record itself. The `arrival_timestamp` is the timestamp attached to the record depending on when the record was received by the processing system.

Data Time Window Batching Model

In the data time window (DTW) batching model, a batch is created for a time window when all records with a `data_timestamp` in that window have been received. Use this batching model when:

- Data is being pulled from (versus being pushed by) the source.
- The extraction logic can filter out records with a `data_timestamp` outside the time window.

For example, use DTW batching when extracting all transactions within a time window from a database. DTW batching makes the analyst's life easier with analytics since there can be a guarantee that all records for a given time window are present in that batch. So, the analyst knows exactly what data they are working with. But DTW batching is not very predictable since out-of-order records could result in delays.

Arrival Time Window Batching Model

In the arrival time window (ATW) batching model, a batch is created at a certain wall-clock time with records that were received in the time window prior to that time. Use this batching model when:

- Records in a batch can be received out of order; i.e., they can have `data_timestamps` that are outside the arrival time window.
- The volume of records is really high.

ATW batching is more predictable since batches are created based on wall-clock time without having to wait for all records for a given time window. This predictability allows for more robust resource allocation and tolerance for failures.

In this case, the analyst will have to query multiple batches to guarantee that all records with `data_timestamps` in the given time window are included. But in cases where 100% accuracy is not essential, ATW batching is sufficient. For example, when analyzing daily active users of a consumer internet company by querying usage logs, the margin of error caused by out-of-order records may be acceptable.

ATW and DTW Batching in the Same Pipeline

It is not a mutually exclusive decision to use DTW versus ATW batching. For example, consider a set of records that arrive at different times, as shown in the following `arrival_time_table`. Start with ATW batching for robustness. Records with `data_timestamps` in the same time window are actually batched into separate batches.

Based on how much delay there might be in records—let's say, three hours— a step in the pipeline called *close of books* can be performed. This step creates a batch of data for the 23rd hour by looking for rows in the next few batches.

The subsequent query is run at a wall-clock time with a delay of three hours (2020/07/24 03:00) because we may have received records until then with a `data_timestamp` in the hour time window of 2020/07/23 23:00.

The `closed_books_table` for the 23rd hour has all rows for that hour. So, `closed_books_table` is a DTW batched table. The analyst can query this batch and be guaranteed that their analysis is complete for the 23rd hour.

---

arrival_time_table

recordid	data_timestamp	arrival_timestamp	batch_timelabel
1	2020/07/23 23:51	2020/07/23 23:55	2020/07/23 23:00
2	2020/07/23 23:46	2020/07/23 23:59	
3	2020/07/23 23:46	2020/07/24 00:00	2020/07/24 00:00
4	2020/07/24 00:15	2020/07/24 00:33	
5	2020/07/24 00:20	2020/07/24 00:45	
6	2020/07/23 23:36	2020/07/24 00:51	
7	2020/07/24 00:36	2020/07/24 01:06	2020/07/24 01:00
8	2020/07/23 00:36	2020/07/24 01:07	
9	2020/07/24 01:05	2020/07/24 00:59	

```
Select *
from arrival_time_table
where data_timestamp > '2020/07/23 23:00'
and data_timestamp < '2020/07/24 00:00'
```

closed_books_table

recordid	data_timestamp	arrival_timestamp	batch_timelabel	closed_books_timelabel
1	2020/07/23 23:51	2020/07/23 23:55	2020/07/23 23:00	2020/07/24 02:00
2	2020/07/23 23:46	2020/07/23 23:59		
3	2020/07/23 23:46	2020/07/24 00:00		
6	2020/07/23 23:36	2020/07/24 00:51		
8	2020/07/23 23:36	2020/07/24 01:07		
12	2020/07/24 23:45	2020/07/24 02:30		

This example shows that the trade-offs around completeness and latency requirements can be incorporated into the same data pipeline. Analysts can then make an informed decision on when to perform the analysis, before or after closing books. They can choose to query the `arrival_time_table` to get answers with lower latency or they can query the `closed_books_table` to get complete answers.

Beware of Silver-Bullet Syndrome

Thomas Nield

Technology job postings often describe the need for passionate people who work hard and strongly advocate their ideas. After all, Steve Jobs was passionate, so maybe that is a trait of successful people!

But in the data engineering and analytics world, passionate people often have a strong opinion about using a certain platform. We all have encountered this person: the one who zealously promotes Apache Spark or pushes to have all data wrangling work done in Alteryx Designer. There is a strong emphasis on the tool and not so much on the problem/solution pairing.

Sometimes this behavior is driven by a desire for standardization and to simplify hiring, which is certainly valid. But more often than not, I have seen people zealously advocate a tool simply because they were passionate about it or, even worse, built their professional identity around it.

To put it simply, it is never a good idea to build your professional identity around a tool. Tools and applications come and go, and what is hot today may be deprecated tomorrow. This alone should give you reason to pause before advocating a technology too quickly. Ask anyone who has done JavaScript (*https://oreil.ly/I7JtN*).

Another reason that over-advocating a tool is a bad idea is best described by the expression "When all you have is a hammer, everything starts to look like a nail." More than once in my career, I have had difficult problems land on my lap that required highly unconventional solutions. While I had thrilled customers, I sometimes had a colleague who wondered why I did not use a preferred/conventional tool to solve it. I had to point out the irony of asking for a conventional solution to an unconventional problem.

Hadi Hariri at JetBrains best described this behavior as the silver-bullet syndrome (*https://oreil.ly/GchBO*): we expect a single tool to solve all our problems, only to chase the next tool when we are disappointed. Do not fall victim to silver-bullet syndrome and become too passionate about a platform or tool.

Instead, stand back. Be impartial and objective. Realize that different tools may be warranted for different types of problems. Granted, you should strive to standardize tools as much as you can in your workplace, but not at the cost of efficacy.

Do you really want your professional identity to be simply a tool stack? Would you rather your resume say, "I know SQL, MongoDB, and Tableau" or "I am an adaptable professional who can navigate ambiguous environments, overcome departmental barriers, and provide technical insights to maximize data value for an organization"? Build your professional identity on skills, problem-solving, and adaptability—not a fleeting technology.

Building a Career as a Data Engineer

Vijay Kiran

Organizations across every sector are realizing the importance of data and maintaining strong data operations. Its recognition as a powerful business asset has seen the emergence of dedicated data teams comprising full-time roles for data scientists, architects, analysts, and, crucially, data engineers. In this chapter, we'll take a look at how aspiring professionals can take that all-important step onto the data engineer career ladder.

Data engineering encompasses many overlapping disciplines. It is hard to chart a single route to becoming a data engineer. Studies in areas like information and communications technology (ICT) or software engineering will help, but I've also seen amazing data engineers with degrees in physics and mathematics. Career paths are also varied. Strong data engineers on my team have joined from roles as diverse as sales, operations, and even marketing. As long as you have basic experience in writing small scripts and running data-cleansing projects, you should be ready to take your first steps into the world of data engineering.

So, if background isn't so important, what are some of the skills an aspiring data engineer needs to succeed? Three standout skills will give you an important head start.

The first of these is solid experience across the software development life cycle. I may be a bit biased here, given my own background as a software engineer, but the skills that working across a software development life cycle gives you are invaluable in the world of data engineering.

Second is knowledge of how to properly use SQL, as well as a good grasp of at least one other static and one dynamic programming language. This might seem basic, but it can't be overstated just how much organizations rely on SQL in their data operations. Combining this with an understanding of how to work with, for example, Python and Rust will give you an important grasp of how great software is built and, ultimately, how it can be applied to the world of data.

The third foundational skill is dependent on the subrole of data engineering you want to specialize in. For those looking to specialize in data processing, developing your understanding of data storage technologies, as well as continuing to hone your skills with SQL, is key. For those who want to go down a more traditional software engineering route, honing your analytical skills will be crucial, as your main focus will be on big data projects. The bottom line here is that you should decide early on which area you want to focus on and develop your skills to complement that function.

My final piece of advice applies to every level, from aspiring data engineers through to established software engineers looking to take the next step up: get into open source! If you're learning how to build and having fun with open source data engineering, you're adding to your repertoire of skills. The best way to get ahead in your data engineering career is to start using open source tools.

Business Dashboards for Data Pipelines

Valliappa (Lak) Lakshmanan

Show them the data; they'll tell you when it's wrong.

When you build data pipelines to ingest data, how often are you not quite sure whether you are processing the data correctly? Are the outliers you are clipping really a result of malfunctioning equipment? Is the timestamp really in Coordinated Universal Time (UTC)? Is a certain field populated only if the customer accepts the order?

If you are diligent, you will ask a stakeholder these questions at the time you are building the pipeline. But what about the questions you didn't know you had to ask? What if the answer changes next month?

One of the best ways to get many eyes, especially eyes that belong to domain experts, continually on your data pipeline is to build a visual representation of the data flowing through it.[1] By this, I don't mean the engineering bits— not the amount of data flowing through, the number of errors, or the number of connections. You should build a visual representation of the *business data* flowing through. The following is an example of such a dashboard.

---

1 You can find more tips on building data science pipelines in my book *Data Science on the Google Cloud Platform* (*https://oreil.ly/ULpVK*) (O'Reilly).

Build a dashboard showing aspects of your data that your stakeholders find meaningful. For example, show the number of times a particular piece of equipment malfunctioned in the past and whether it is malfunctioning now. To figure this out, you will use the number of outliers that you were clipping out of your data pipeline. Build the dashboard, share it widely, and wait.

People are drawn to real-time dashboards like cats are to catnip. The day that those outlier values are produced for some reason other than malfunctioning equipment, someone will call you and let you know.

This works only if the dashboard in question is web-based or integrated into the everyday systems that decision makers use. You can use free dashboard tools like Data Studio, or tools like Tableau and Looker that have free tiers. Learn how to use them to spread your semantic burden.

Caution: Data Science Projects Can Turn into the Emperor's New Clothes

Shweta Katre

The fourth industrial revolution has dawned: the *Age of Analytics*. There is a mad rush to develop predictive models and algorithms to establish supremacy in an immensely competitive, data-driven world. Starting off with predictive analytics and moving into the realm of machine learning and artificial intelligence, most companies are expanding their capabilities to spawn data science projects.

Enormous pressure is placed on data science teams, like all other kinds of project teams, to deliver business value that is usable and potentially releasable in a specific time frame. A big challenge for data science teams is to show visible and measurable progress/work done, to keep stakeholder interest alive and the funding steady.

However, roughly 80% of project time is spent on data collection/selection, data preparation, and exploratory analysis (see the following figure). Project overheads are huge, but there is no visible output. The promised predictive model or algorithm is not revealed in the early or even middle stages. Sometimes, in the evaluation or validation stage, the possibility arises of scrapping the entire analysis and going back to the drawing board. In such scenarios, resources have been used up, hours have been burned, but no output has resulted—à la the emperor's new clothes!

How do you save your data science team from the emperor embarrassment? Data science projects call for strategic planning and management of priorities, resources, and infrastructure, as outlined in these steps:

1. Understand the *sell-first approach*. What basic need were the stakeholders promised your project would meet? The IT industry is moving away from full big-bang deployments. It's all about iterations. No matter how

many data sources we scour, or which cutting-edge technology we showcase, data science release road maps should be designed in such a way that every iteration pushes the fulfillment of that very basic need in some direction.

2. Give a "face" to the project. Not only for the stakeholders but also from a project manager or product owner's perspective, there needs to be a window into what's going on. A user interface (UI) that acts as a face for under-the-hood analytics can help visualize the analytics process and give insight into the project's progress. This UI or dashboard should be interactive and identify the specific datasets being utilized and the exact model used to obtain a specific result set. It can also be used for validation and acceptance among the user group.

3. Ensure environment readiness. The development environment should be capable of quickly populating databases and changing datasets for exploratory analysis. Memory management issues are major blockers to most data science projects. Huge amounts of data will be downloaded from various data sources. They could be shapefiles, spreadsheets, or text files. An effective memory management plan for all computing and storage devices in the development environment should be in place.

4. Catalog scripts. Scripts for downloading data, scripts for data cleansing and preparation, and scripts for data archiving should be tagged appropriately for reuse.

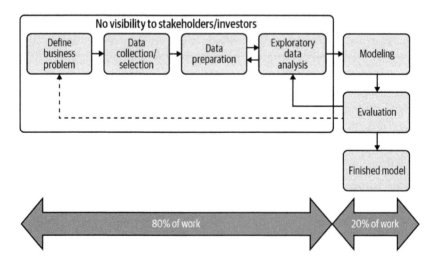

The data science ecosystem can consist of a diverse data science team, diverse tool sets, and a variety of data. It's the end goal of the project that ties all the analytics effort together. It could result in the formulation of a clever algorithm for AI, or it could result in a failure. Either way, the outcome of steps 1 through 4 will ensure that our stakeholders do not lose faith in our efforts and we do not produce a high-tech version of the emperor's new clothes!

Change Data Capture

Raghotham Murthy

Change data capture (CDC) is a solution to a specific problem. You have your most valuable data in your production databases. You want to analyze that data, but you don't want to add any more load to those production databases. Instead, you want to rely on a data warehouse or data lake. Once you decide that you want to analyze data from your production database in a different system, you need a reliable way to replicate that data from the production database to your data warehouse.

It turns out, at scale, this is a hard problem to solve. You can't just decide to copy data over from the production database to the warehouse—that would add a lot more load on the production database, especially if you want high fidelity. And if you fetched only the changed records, you would miss deletes.

Thankfully, all modern production databases write out a *write-ahead log* (WAL), or *change log*, as part of their normal transaction processing. This log captures every single change to each row/cell in each table in the database and can be used in database replication to create replicas of the production database. In CDC, a tool reads this write-ahead log and applies the changes to the data warehouse. This technique is a lot more robust than batch exports of the tables and has a low footprint on the production database.

However, you have to treat CDC as an end-to-end data pipeline in order to correctly replicate data initially as well as on an ongoing basis. You need to consider several aspects of the CDC connector life cycle. Here are a few examples:

Scale
> The CDC pipeline has to be robust enough for high data volume. For example, in PostgreSQL, delays in reading the WAL can cause the database's disk space to run out!

Replication lag
> This refers to the duration between the time that a transaction is committed in the primary database and the time it becomes available in the

data warehouse. You have to build checks to make sure that your pipeline is minimizing lag time before transformations are run.

Schema changes

Over time, database schemas evolve because tables or columns are added or removed or types are updated. It is important to propagate the schema changes to the data warehouse. Sometimes a schema change might require a historical sync.

Masking

You have to mask sensitive columns for compliance purposes.

Historical syncs

Before applying the CDC changes, an initial historical sync of the tables is needed. It can take a while and can overload the source. It's better to do historical syncs from a replica database to speed them up and reduce load on the primary database. Sometimes partial interruptions might occur in the WAL, so you need partial historical syncs instead of full historical syncs to recover fast.

There are typically no strong reasons to build your own CDC connectors. Use existing tools instead!

Column Names as Contracts

Emily Riederer

Software products use unit tests and service-level agreements (SLAs) to make performance promises; interfaces have common symbols and labels. However, data tables exist somewhere in between—neither engineered like a service nor designed like an application. This lack of conversation and contract-making between producers and consumers leaves engineers confused about why users aren't satisfied (or make vague complaints of "data quality") and consumers befuddled that the data is never quite "right."

Using a controlled vocabulary for naming fields in published datasets is a low-tech, low-friction solution to this dilemma. Developing a common language forms a shared understanding of how each field in a dataset is intended to work, and it can also alleviate producer overhead in data validation, documentation, and wrangling.

Engineers and analysts can define up front a tiered set of stubs with atomic, well-defined meanings. When pieced together, these stubs can be used to describe complex metrics and behaviors.

Imagine you work at a ride-share company and are building a data table with one record per trip. What might a controlled vocabulary look like?

A first level might characterize different measures, consisting of both a data type (e.g., `bool` or `int`) and appropriate usage patterns. For example:

ID
> Integer. Non-null. Unique identifier for an entity. Likely a primary key.

IND
> Binary. Non-null. Indicator of an event occurrence.

N
> Integer. Non-null. Non-negative count of quantity of event occurrences.

AMT

Numeric. Summable, continuous "denominator-free" amount.

VAL

Numeric. Not inherently summable (e.g., a rate, ratio, latitude, or longitude).

DT

Date. Always in YYYY-MM-DD form.

TM

Timestamp.

The second level might characterize the *subject* of the measure, such as a DRIVER, RIDER, TRIP, ORIG, or DEST. Additional levels would provide additional "adjectives" to modify the measure subjects. For example, we might have CITY, ZIP, LAT, and LON.

Altogether, this structure provides a grammar to concisely characterize a wide range of metrics. Isn't it fairly self-evident what ID_DRIVER, TM_ORIG, VAL_DEST_LON, and IND_TRIP_SURGE mean?

Not only do these names provide a nice interface for users, but they disambiguate data requirements in important ways that can help directly automate data management tasks. Metadata management and data discoverability tasks can be partially automated by reconstructing variable definitions from stubs (e.g., "unique identifier of a ride-share driver") and allowing users to easily search all tables for a given set of concepts (all timestamps, everything to do with a trip's origin). Similarly, performance contracts promised to users in the top-level stubs can translate seamlessly to automated data-validation checks ("everything that starts with DT should be cast as a date," "nothing in AMT fields should be a decimal," "IND variables must not be null") in tools like Great Expectations. Finally, such variables may prove useful mental guides in your own further munging (e.g., "it doesn't make sense to sum up VAL variables").

Of course, no single, silver-bullet solution exists for data quality, discoverability, and communication. But using column names to form contracts is a useful way to start communicating both with your users and your workflow tools.

Consensual, Privacy-Aware Data Collection

Katharine Jarmul

How consensual is your data collection? Are customers aware of how their data is being used? Do they know how it is transformed, aggregated, fed into a model, and deployed? Is it being done with respect for their privacy? Can they ask for it not to be included in any of those automated processes? Do you have privacy-protection mechanisms to ensure that sensitive data is not at risk?

As data engineers, we aim for precision and efficiency. How can we get data from place A to place B, with the necessary in-between steps for cleaning, testing, and validation, and how can we do that most efficiently?

What gets lost in this objective to expedite and automate processing is that we are often handling personal data—sometimes extremely sensitive data. And if you've had the pleasure of working with European Union (EU) residents' data, you might have thought about these topics further because of the General Data Protection Regulation (GDPR). How can we remove artifacts from users whose data we no longer have rights to? What does it mean for a person to be subject to automated processing? What does consensual data collection look like?

If we want to collect data consensually—for all people, not just those lucky enough to reside in the EU—we need to fundamentally change some of the ways we move data. Here are some ideas on how we can get started.

Attach Consent Metadata

We can do this as part of our processing. We have the means to determine who this user is and what they consented to or opted out of. We can filter or reroute their data depending on their level of consent. This means we can also implement better user experiences for those who want to opt out of some processing (i.e., slightly less awful cookie alerts!).

Track Data Provenance

Do you know where all your data came from? Unfortunately, for many of us, the answer is no. Tracking data provenance not only allows for better understanding of legal and privacy-related concerns, but also helps us determine data quality and what processing might have been applied to the data before it got to us. It's a win-win!

Drop or Encrypt Sensitive Fields

We should apply data-protection mechanisms when we know the sensitive fields our data may contain. Do we really need usernames for aggregate analytics? Nope? Then drop them (or don't collect them in the first place). Do we need email addresses for our chatbot training? Nope? Then make sure they don't make it into the model. As data engineers, we can apply our knowledge and tools to ensure that sensitive data is protected.

Many of us take a variety of measures to protect the privacy of ourselves and our loved ones. Extend the courtesy to the customers and users of the products you create by implementing consensual data collection and basic data-privacy measures.

Cultivate Good Working Relationships with Data Consumers

Ido Shlomo

The relationship between data engineers and data consumers—whether they're data scientists, business intelligence (BI) teams, or one of a multitude of analytics teams—is always complex. All of these functions exist to serve the overall data-driven goals of the organization and are expected to integrate seamlessly. So there is clear motivation to cooperate, but more often than not, the division of labor is far from balanced—a situation that can develop into real tension between the teams.

There is no recipe for creating a perfect symbiotic relationship, and this is doubly true given the great amount of variation in the structure of data teams across organizations. That said, the following points can help data engineers avoid major pitfalls and aim for a better direction.

Don't Let Consumers Solve Engineering Problems

Avoid the temptation of letting data consumers solve data-engineering problems. Many types of data consumers exist, and the core competencies of each individual vary across multiple spectrums—coding skills, statistical knowledge, visualization abilities, and more. In many cases, the more technically capable data consumers will attempt to close infrastructure gaps themselves by applying ad hoc fixes. This can take the form of applying additional data transformations to a pipeline that isn't serving its purpose or even actual infrastructure design.

Superficially, it may appear to the data engineer as a win-win situation: their own time is saved, and the consumer's work proceeds unhindered. However, this usually results in convoluted layers of suboptimal solutions that make the organization's data infrastructure increasingly hard to manage.

Adapt Your Expectations

Avoid applying engineering sensibilities to data consumers. As fully trained developers, data engineers usually follow contemporary programming best practices. These imply stringent coding style and focus on efficiency and unit-test coverage. Some organizations opt for very close-knit data teams or even unify all of the functions inside a single DataOps team.

In such cases, data engineers should tailor their expectations to those of data consumers who work intensively with code but do not follow those best practices. This is usually not motivated by ignorance on their part, but is rather adherence to their primary business function, which requires that they prioritize other things.

Understand Consumers' Jobs

Put a premium on knowing what data consumers actually do. Data consumers rely on data infrastructure to do their respective jobs. Their level of comfort, productivity, and adoption depends on the fit between that infrastructure and the dynamics of their work. Data engineers are tasked with developing this infrastructure from conception to implementation, and the actual day-to-day needs of the respective consumers are therefore critical context.

This usually implies spending both time and effort to get a clear read, whether in the form of shadowing sessions, iterative proofs of concept (POCs), or both low- and high-level ideation discussions. The increase in professional familiarity between the teams also leads to an increase in mutual respect and amiability, and that in itself is a powerful driver of success.

Data Engineering != Spark

Jesse Anderson

The misconception that Apache Spark is all you'll need for your data pipeline (*https://oreil.ly/SY8Sk*) is common.[1] The reality is that you're going to need components from three general types of technologies to create a data pipeline. These three general types of big data technologies are:

- Computation
- Storage
- Messaging

Fixing and remedying this misconception is crucial to success with big data projects or one's own learning about big data. Spark is just one part of a larger big data ecosystem that's necessary to create data pipelines.

Put another way:

> *Data Engineering = Computation + Storage + Messaging + Coding + Architecture + Domain Knowledge + Use Cases*

Batch and Real-Time Systems

Generally, you have to solve two core problems in a batch data pipeline. The first is computation, and the second is the storage of data. Spark is a good solution for handling batch computation, but it can be more difficult to find the right storage sollution—or more correctly, too identify the different and optimized storage technologies for your use case.

Computation Component

Computation is how your data gets processed. Computation frameworks are responsible for running the algorithms and the majority of your code. For

---

1 A version of this chapter was originally published at *jesse-anderson.com*.

big data, they're responsible for resource allocation, running the code in a distributed fashion, and persisting the results.

Storage Component

Storage is how your data gets persisted permanently. For simple storage requirements, people will just dump their files into a directory. As the requirements become slightly more difficult, we start to use partitioning. This will put files in directories with specific names. A common partitioning method is to use the date of the data as part of the directory name.

NoSQL Databases

For more optimized storage requirements, we start using *NoSQL databases*. The need for NoSQL databases is especially prevalent when you have a real-time system. Most companies store data in both a simple storage technology and one or more NoSQL databases. Storing data multiple times accomodates the different use cases or read/write patterns that are necessary. One application may need to read everything, and another application may need only specific data.

Messaging Component

Messaging is how knowledge or events get passed in real time. You start to use messaging when there is a need for real-time systems (*https://oreil.ly/7MWu6*). These messaging frameworks are used to ingest and disseminate a large amount of data. This ingestion and dissemination is crucial to real-time systems because it solves the first-mile and last-mile problems (*https://oreil.ly/rkrrF*).

Data Engineering for Autonomy and Rapid Innovation

Jeff Magnusson

In many organizations, data engineering is treated purely as a specialty. Data pipelines are seen as the complex, arcane domain of data engineers. Often data engineers are organized into dedicated teams, or embedded into vertically oriented product-based teams.

While delegating work to specialists often makes sense, it also implies that a handoff is required in order to accomplish something that spans beyond that specialty. Fortunately, with the right frameworks and infrastructure in place, handoffs are unnecessary to accomplish (and, perhaps more importantly, iterate on!) many data flows and tasks.

Data pipelines can generally be decomposed into business or algorithmic logic (metric computation, model training, featurization, etc.) and data-flow logic (complex joins, data wrangling, sessionization, etc.). Data engineers specialize in implementing data-flow logic, but often must implement other logic to spec based on the desires or needs of the team requesting the work, and without the ability to autonomously adjust those requirements.

This happens because both types of logic are typically intertwined and implemented hand-in-hand throughout the pipelines. Instead, look for ways to decouple data-flow logic from other forms of logic within the pipeline. Here are some strategies.

Implement Reusable Patterns in the ETL Framework

Rather than turning common patterns into templates, implement them as functions within an ETL framework. This minimizes code skew and maintenance burden, and makes data pipelines more accessible to contributors beyond the data-engineering team.

Choose a Framework and Tool Set Accessible Within the Organization

One reason data engineering is viewed as a specialty is that data pipelines are often implemented in a language or tool set that is not common to the rest of the organization. Consider adopting a framework that supports a language that is widely known and used within your organization (hint: SQL is widely known and understood outside the data-engineering specialty).

Move the Logic to the Edges of the Pipelines

Look to move data-flow logic as far upstream or downstream as possible. This allows the remainder of the work to happen as a pre- or post-processing step, effectively decoupling the data engineers from data consumers, and restoring autonomy to iterate without further handoffs.

Create and Support Staging Tables

Staging tables are often employed as intermediate checkpoints or outputs between jobs in data pipelines. However, they are often treated as ephemeral datasets used only by the pipeline they run in. If you need to implement a tricky or expensive join or processing step, consider staging out the results and supporting their use by other, less specialized folks within the organization.

Bake Data-Flow Logic into Tooling and Infrastructure

Bake common patterns into frameworks or tooling that is invoked via configuration. Data-engineering logic can often be highly leveraged by pushing it into data acquisition, access, or storage code. Rather than expressing the configuration of data-flow logic within data pipelines, consider embedding it in the metadata store as metadata on input or output data sources.

Data Engineering from a Data Scientist's Perspective

Bill Franks

People have focused on the ingestion and management of data for decades, but only recently has data engineering become a widespread role.[1] Why is that? This chapter offers a somewhat contrarian view.

Database Administration, ETL, and Such

Historically, people working with enterprise data focused on three primary areas. First were those who manage raw data collection into source systems. Second were those focused on ETL operations. Until recently, ETL roles were overwhelmingly focused on relational databases. Third were database administrators who manage those relational systems.

The work of these traditional data roles is largely standardized. For example, database administrators don't tell a database which disks to store data on or how to ensure relational integrity. Since relational technology is mature, many complex tasks are easy. Similarly, ETL tools have adapters for common source systems, functionality to handle common transformation operations, and hooks into common destination repositories. For years, a small number of mature tools interfaced with a small number of mature data repositories. Life was relatively simple!

---

1 This chapter is based on a post published on the International Institute for Analytics (*https://oreil.ly/BkxZo*) blog.

Why the Need for Data Engineers?

The roles described previously still exist today in their traditional states. However, those roles are no longer sufficient. Data engineers have stepped in to fill the void.

Today, we have many new data types that aren't friendly to ETL tools or relational databases, and so new tools are needed. However, most of these new tools and repositories are not yet mature and require complex coding. Worse, it is often necessary to integrate multiple immature technologies.

Data engineers figure out how to do this integration, often with few documented examples. It takes hard work to get the pieces of a data pipeline to work together efficiently and securely, and it often requires more energy input and complexity than should be needed.

Adding even more complexity are architectures spanning internal systems and external cloud environments. Outsiders say, "Just pull that data together for us; what's the holdup?" But, alas, tasks can be simple to define yet difficult to execute.

There are differences between data engineers and traditional data professionals. First, data engineers need to be more skilled at creative problem solving. Next, data engineers need to embrace and use an ever-wider array of tools and approaches. Last, data engineers must focus on integration and optimization across tools and platforms as opposed to optimizing workloads within a given tool or platform.

What's the Future?

Much of what data engineers do today via brute force will become standardized over time. This illustrates a parallel between data science and data engineering. A lot of what used to take a data scientist's time is being automated and standardized. "Citizen data scientists" now handle a lot, while data scientists focus on harder problems. We will soon see "citizen data engineers" who make use of standardized data-engineering tools to handle the basics, while data engineers focus on the new frontiers.

Data Pipeline Design Patterns for Reusability and Extensibility

Mukul Sood

Designing extensible, modular, reusable data pipelines is a large topic that's relevant in data engineering, as it requires dealing with constant change across different layers such as data sources, ingestion, validation, processing, security, logging, and monitoring. These changes happen at varying rates across the layers and impact data pipelines differently depending on the pipeline's level of abstraction and design.

To provide context for the layers of a data pipeline and to start to map the configuration, the pipeline can be seen in a distilled form as comprising Ingestion, Processing, and Result layers. For each layer, we can think in terms of functions that map to functional blocks. The content of the blocks changes depending on the layer requirements. This helps us think in terms of templates and configuration that could represent the pipeline's directed acyclic graph (DAG).

The Ingestion, Processing, and Result layers could be mapped to different loggers and monitors based on requirements. For example, in the Ingestion layer, the file log could be S3, the event log could be custom, and the monitors could be Google Cloud operations and Redash. However, the Results layer could be mapped to a DataDog event log and event monitor.

If we take a generic pipeline, specifically looking at logging and monitoring, this representation would be implemented as DAG methods, where loggers and monitors would be coupled with DAG code. This involves more coding and is brittle, difficult to reuse, and a violation of design principles including the single-responsibility principle (SRP), Don't Repeat Yourself (DRY), and open/closed—making the overall pipeline unstable and unreliable. If we extend this beyond monitoring and logging, we will see similar problems in different functional blocks—data quality/validation, security/privacy, etc.

When we see similarities in problems, that is an indicator to recognize the common themes. In addition, we want to remove the coupling between implementations and increase cohesion within them. This gives us enough context to start thinking in terms of design patterns (refer to *Design Patterns: Elements of Reusable Object-Oriented Software* (*https://en.wikipedia.org/wiki/ Design_Patterns*) by Erich Gamma et al. [Addison-Wesley]).

The first set of patterns are *creational* or *structural*. They allow us to separate creation and structure of cross-cutting concerns such as logging and monitoring from DAG-specific areas. The factory (*https://oreil.ly/c7umN*) and abstract factory (*https://oreil.ly/4E09D*) patterns help in abstracting and decoupling the different loggers and monitors from the DAG code, allowing the DAG codebase to evolve without dependencies on the logging and monitoring codebase.

The second set of patterns are *behavioral*. They allow us to specify behavior while maintaining DRY and SOLID principles. The decorator (*https:// oreil.ly/q5tAU*) pattern is widely used to modify or add behavior to existing functions. Logging and monitoring are immediately applicable.

The facade (*https://oreil.ly/SFHb6*) pattern is useful when a narrower or specific API is needed for the client or consumer. For example, the broad set of APIs or methods exposed by the different loggers and monitors do not need to be exposed to the DAG layer. The facade pattern helps define an access or interface to the logging and monitoring layer.

When we combine these patterns, we realize the benefits of design principles, as the separation of responsibilities allows the modularization of the codebase at multiple levels: DAG, cross-cutting concerns (separate packages for monitoring and logging), cross-DAG (common templates can be abstracted). This provides building blocks for generalizing the data pipelines to move away from writing custom code to more generic modules, templates, and configuration. The different pieces follow their own development cycles and deployment packages, completely decoupled from the DAG codebase.

Adding these design principles does increase the level of abstraction and complexity. However, that is a small price to pay for scaling up the pipeline development while maintaining quality and velocity.

Data Quality for Data Engineers

Katharine Jarmul

If you manage and deploy data pipelines, how do you ensure they are working? Do you test that data is going through? Do you monitor uptime? Do you even have tests? If so, what exactly do you test?

Data pipelines aren't too dissimilar to other pipelines in our world (gas, oil, water). They need to be engineered; they have a defined start and end point. They need to be tested for leaks and regularly monitored. But unlike most data pipelines, these "real-world" pipelines also test the quality of what they carry. Regularly.

When was the last time you tested your data pipeline for data quality? When was the last time you validated the schema of the incoming or transformed data, or tested for the appropriate ranges of values (i.e., "common sense" testing)? How do you ensure that low-quality data is either flagged or managed in a meaningful way?

More than ever before—given the growth and use of large-scale data pipelines—data validation, testing, and quality checks are critical to business needs. It doesn't necessarily matter that we collect 1TB of data a day if that data is essentially useless for tasks like data science, machine learning, or business intelligence because of poor quality control.

We need data engineers to operate like other pipeline engineers—to be concerned about and focused on the quality of what's running through their pipelines. Data engineers should coordinate with the data science team or implement standard testing. This can be as simple as schema validation and null checks. Ideally, you could also test for expected value ranges and private or sensitive data exposure, or sample data over time for statistical testing (i.e., testing distributions or other properties the data at large should have).

And the neat thing is, you can use your data knowledge and apply it to these problems. Do you know how many extreme values, anomalies, or outliers your pipeline will expect today? Probably not. But could you? Why, yes, you could. Tracking, monitoring, and inferring the types of errors and quality issues you see in your pipelines or processing is—in and of itself—a meaningful data science task.

So please, don't merely see data coming in and going out and say, "Looks good to me." Take the time to determine what quality and validation measurements make sense for your data source and destination, and set up ways to ensure that you can meet those standards. Not only will your data science and business teams thank you for the increase in data quality and utility, but you can also feel proud of your title: engineer.

Data Security for Data Engineers

Katharine Jarmul

Is your data safe? What about the data you process every day? How do you know? Can you guarantee it?

These questions aren't meant to send you running in fear. Instead, I want you to approach security pragmatically. As data engineers, we're often managing the most valuable company resource. For this reason, it only makes sense that we learn and apply security engineering to our work.

How can we do so? Here are a few tips.

Learn About Security

Most data engineers come from either a computer science or a data science background, so you may not have had exposure to computer and network security concepts. Learn about them by attending security conferences, meetups, and other events. Read up on security best practices for the particular architecture or infrastructure you use. Chat with the IT/DevOps or security folks at your company to hear what measures are already in place. I'm not asking you to become an expert, but I do want you to be informed.

Monitor, Log, and Test Access

Monitor, log, and track access to the machines or containers you use, to the databases or other data repositories you maintain, and to the code and processing systems you contribute to daily. Make sure only credentialed users or machines can access these systems. Create firewall rules (yes, even in the cloud and even with containers) and test them by using a port scanner or ping sweep. Monitor and alert on any unusual access or network behavior.

Encrypt Data

Making sure sensitive data is protected should be one of the key things we do as data engineers. Whenever possible, encrypt data or sensitive fields—both at rest and in transit. According to IBM's 2019 Cost of a Data Breach Report (*https://oreil.ly/mJNdl*), this is one of the best ways to prevent a costly data breach.

Automate Security Tests

Already using CI/CD as part of your data engineering? (If not, please stop reading and go do that right now.) Implement security tests as a part of that deployment. This can be as simple as testing bad credentials, testing for encryption, and testing that the latest security updates for your libraries are being used. The more you automate this testing and can stop and alert for any potential security threats, the safer your processing and pipelines will be.

Ask for Help

If you are lucky enough to have a security team, ask them to help you assess the security of the processing infrastructure, networks, and scripts. If not, see when your company's next external security review is scheduled and ask for time to talk with the experts about measures you can take to provide better security for your data engineering.

This can include pen-testing of data collection endpoints or exposed APIs you use or maintain, or simply a security review of the processing deployment, monitoring, and architecture. Either way, getting expert advice will likely make you feel more confident about the measures you have and those you want to prioritize or implement in the future.

For your particular role or company, there may be even more low-hanging security fruit. Scheduling a regular security sprint into your planning is a great way to stay on top of these issues and improve security over time. When faced with those questions again, you and your team can respond with ease of mind, knowing your data-engineering workflows are secure.

Data Validation Is More Than Summary Statistics

Emily Riederer

Which of these numbers doesn't belong? −1, 0, 1, NA.

It may be hard to tell. If the data in question should be non-negative, −1 is clearly wrong; if it should be complete, the NA is problematic; if it represents the signs to be used in summation, 0 is questionable. In short, there is no data quality without *data context*.

Data-quality management is widely recognized as a critical component of data engineering. However, while the need for always-on validation is uncontroversial, approaches vary widely. Too often, these approaches rely solely on summary statistics or basic, univariate anomaly-detection methods that are easily automated and widely scalable. However, in the long run, context-free data-quality checks ignore the nuance and help us detect more-pernicious errors that may go undetected by downstream users.

Defining context-enriched *business rules* as checks on data quality can complement statistical approaches to data validation by encoding domain knowledge. Instead of just defining high-level requirements (e.g., "non-null"), we can define expected interactions between different fields in our data (e.g., "lifetime payments are less than lifetime purchases for each ecommerce customer").

This enables the exploration of internal consistency across fields in one or more datasets—not just the reasonableness of any given field in isolation—and allows us to validate that the data produced concurs with the true business intent (e.g., the aforementioned check is definitely true only if we are considering gross purchases and deducting any returns). While these checks can still be simple arithmetic, they encode a level of intuition that no autonomous approach could hope to find (e.g., the need to compare running totals of select metrics after grouping the data at the customer level) and ask questions that might be more representative of the way our ETL process could break (e.g., by loading payments multiple times).

Business-rule data checks can further exploit unique human knowledge about the data structures that might not be fully evident from the data itself. For example, if we are working with repeated measures (panel) data for a consistent set of subjects, many intended unique keys or expected trends may exist within each subject but not across the whole dataset; alternatively, if we are working with hierarchical data, checks can explore the appropriate "nesting" of these levels.

While context-enriched checks on data quality can help provide a more robust and nuanced validation of data quality, there is no free lunch. The major downside of this approach is that it may require a significant amount of manual work from both the business and engineering teams to define and implement such conditions. As such, developers must carefully prioritize where to invest limited resources. However, even adding these checks to particularly critical subsets of fields or especially error-prone steps in a pipeline (major transformations or combinations of diverse sources) can go a long way toward promoting a more holistic approach to data quality.

Data Warehouses Are the Past, Present, and Future

James Densmore

The death of the data warehouse, long prophesied, seems to be always on the horizon yet never realized. First it was NoSQL, then Hadoop, then data lakes that would kill the data warehouse. Yet here we are. Snowflake was the hottest initial public offering (IPO) of 2020, and the demand for data and analytics engineers who can crank value out of a data warehouse is as high as ever.

In 2010, the future of data warehouses felt pretty bleak. Most analytics teams were relying on traditional row-based, online transactional processing (OLTP) databases for their data warehouses. Data volume was exploding. When it came to processing and querying all that data for analysis, columnar databases came to the rescue, but they required expanding hardware.

While data warehouse bare-metal appliances provided a massive jump in processing power, it was quite an investment to add the hardware to your server room. It's unimaginable 10 years later.

Things changed for the better in 2012, when Amazon launched Redshift, a columnar data warehouse that you could spin up in minutes and pay for in small increments with no massive up-front cost, built on top of PostgreSQL.

Migrations away from overtaxed, row-based SQL data warehouses to Redshift grew massively. The barrier to entry for a high-performing data warehouse was lowered substantially, and suddenly what looked like the impending death of the warehouses was a rebirth.

Next, extract, load, transform (ELT) wiped out extract, transform, load (ETL). The difference between the two patterns is where the T (transform) step takes place, and distributed columnar databases made it all possible. It's now better to focus on extracting data and loading it into a data warehouse, and then performing the necessary transformations. With ELT, data engineers can focus on the extract and load steps, while analysts can utilize SQL to transform the data that's been ingested for reporting and analysis.

In other words, this new breed of data warehouses made it possible (and economical) to store and query far higher volumes of data than ever before. ELT saved the data warehouse.

The concept of a data lake was first introduced in 2011. The benefit of storing vast amounts of data without having to define its structure when it's stored (schema-on-write), but rather when it's queried (schema-on-read), is real. However, there's a cost to such an approach when it comes to data discovery and governance, as well as in complexity for the data analytics or analytics engineer who works with the data.

With the cost of storing and querying large structured datasets dropping and the performance spiking upward, some of the downsides of data lakes for analytics became more noticeable. Still, data lakes have a place in an analytics infrastructure. There's still a need to store data that's not consistently structured, or in a volume that makes even the most robust data warehouses creak. However, for most data teams, data lakes have been a complement to their data warehouse rather than a replacement.

Data warehouses aren't going anywhere anytime soon. Snowflake continues to blow away expectations for developers and investors alike, and I expect a wave of data warehouse innovation in the near future.

For those hesitant to invest in a greenfield data warehouse, migrate a legacy one to a modern platform, or hire data engineers with data warehousing know-how, don't fear! You're building for now and investing intelligently for the future.

Defining and Managing Messages in Log-Centric Architectures

Boris Lublinsky

Messaging systems are changing the way we are exposing data. Instead of focusing on the API between a producer and consumer, we have to focus on the message definitions.

With logs becoming a centerpiece of the architecture, they are starting to take on the role of an enterprise data backbone (*https://oreil.ly/XCI3F*), somewhat similar to the Hadoop Distributed File System (HDFS (*https://oreil.ly/ytjFn*)) for streaming systems. This architecture encourages the creation of canonical data models, because schema enforcement avoids many problems (e.g., typing errors). This is not a new idea—compare it to the canonical data model (*https://oreil.ly/1YsxA*) used in enterprise application integration (EAI) and service-oriented architecture (SOA), and the concept of standardized service contracts (*https://oreil.ly/aDUXD*). The rationale is the same in both cases, and this approach is identical to the EAI canonical messaging pattern (*https://oreil.ly/8snL5*), ensuring that the content of the log will be understood by all participants.

The canonical data model provides an additional level of decoupling between each service's individual data format and simplifies data mapping among internal models of different services. If a new service is added to the implementation, only a transformation between the canonical data model and the internal model is required, independent of how this data is represented by other services using it.

Ideally, this canonical data model should never change, but in reality it does. In these cases, you should strive for backward compatibility when making changes to message schemas for services that produce messages. Sometimes breaking changes are unavoidable. In this case, existing consumers of the given message schema are at risk of breaking.

A solution to this problem, similar to API versioning best practices (*https:// oreil.ly/WmWcV*), is creation of a new deployment of the service with a new topic. Consumers that support the new schema can consume messages from this topic, while the ones that assume an old schema will continue to leverage existing ones.

This approach to versioning allows functionality to evolve independently without breaking the rest of the system. A downside of this approach is increased size and complexity of the overall system, caused by multiple deployments of the same service with different versions. To prevent this from happening, it is important to introduce a version-deprecation policy; old versions should be deleted after a set time period.

Message design and management are important components of log-centric architecture. To build your system correctly, make sure that you leverage the following:

- A well-defined semantic data model that is the foundation of your message definitions.
- A well-defined strategy allowing easy creation and deletion of topics to support versioning. It is also recommended to directly encode a version identifier into the topic name.

Demystify the Source and Illuminate the Data Pipeline

Meghan Kwartler

You've been assigned to a new project, new team, or new company. You want to dig in and make an impact to add business value. It can be tempting to start writing code immediately, but if you resist the inclination to make initial assumptions and instead give your attention to setting up a solid foundation, it will pay dividends moving forward.

First, discover where and how the data originates. When your data is initiated from users, it is useful to get their perspective on their entry experience. Each time I walk the floor of a manufacturing plant or talk to a machine operator about how they use a system, I gain valuable knowledge. Often I discover ways users are entering data that are inconsistent with the original system design, or the valid reasons why they are omitting data. If you don't have access to the people entering data, study their training documentation and talk to the business analysts associated with that function.

Get to know the specifications when your data originates from sensors, equipment, or hardware. Dig into the manuals and documentation to clarify how the data is generated. You will then have a clear understanding when you encounter this data later in your analysis. Knowing the expected values also helps you identify possible malfunctions in the source equipment.

Now examine the metadata. You have discovered the originating business events for implicit, explicit, manually entered, or automatically generated data. Descriptive metadata accompanies each of these sources. For example, metadata includes equipment event timestamps, device types, or descriptive user data. Determine whether this metadata from numerous sources is consistent and could be unified. For instance, timestamp formatting may differ across time zones.

Now it's time to trace. Whether you've identified one or one hundred sources of data, how does that data move through the pipeline and arrive in the place where you will access it? Another consideration is that data types could be converted, and business translation may be required as data moves through systems.

If you have the good fortune to receive this type of information during your onboarding, be extremely grateful and recognize that this documentation is a gift. It will set you up for success. Then reference it. Sometimes effort is made to develop valuable documentation, but more often it isn't utilized to its fullest capacity.

During your investigation, create documentation if it doesn't exist. It doesn't need to be overly complicated. It can be simple and yet make a strong impact at the same time. Pay it forward and help the next person who will be tasked with using data to benefit the business.

Develop Communities, Not Just Code

Emily Riederer

As a data engineer, you may think of your core job responsibility as building a data pipeline. In fact, that's probably what was laid out in your job description and how your value is measured by your manager. However, you're uniquely positioned to exercise a much greater impact on your organization if you think about developing a *data culture* along with your *data products*.

The data you produce is likely consumed by countless data scientists, data analysts, and users spread across disparate lines of business. In large organizations, these individuals may be fragmented and unaware of similar questions they are asking and answering with the same core data assets. In this sense, your data is posed to be a shared platform that can connect a network of users with common objectives. Empowered users not only will derive more value from your data, but also may be able to self-service or crowd-source more of their data needs instead of continuing to rely on a data-engineering team for ad hoc requests.

Such networks and communities won't arise without concerted effort. Downstream users are typically focused on obtaining answers to specific business and strategy questions and see data as a means to an end—not a central, binding force in an analytical ecosystem. Additionally, the data literacy and proficiency of data consumers across different tools may cause more fragmentation.

Data scientists may be adept at Spark or have all their code in Jupyter notebooks on GitHub, whereas line-of-business users might struggle with SQL and resort to dashboards, spreadsheets, or canned reports for their data needs. The confluence of tight timelines, matrixed organizations, and disparate tools leaves your users without a shared language or forum to find commonalities.

Here are some ways you can help foster a data community or practice:

- Query usage logs and, when privacy permits, publish them to help users connect.

- Engage with users to understand what business questions bring them to your data and how they interact with it. This can be done in individual one-on-one user interviews or larger design sessions.

- Empower users by providing training and resources for them to engage with data in more advanced ways. Don't underestimate that what you perceive as basic skills could be transformative. For example, teaching a marketing team basic SQL or training data scientists in Airflow could help these teams automate parts of their workflows.

- Share as much of your work as possible (e.g., scripts that are part of your ETL pipeline) to help more-advanced users learn and reuse them.

- Build centralized tools that help users consume data, and open them to community contribution.

Effective Data Engineering in the Cloud World

Dipti Borkar

VP of Product, Alluxio

The cloud has changed the dynamics of data engineering as well as the behavior of data engineers in many ways. This is primarily because a data engineer on premises deals only with databases and some parts of the Hadoop stack. In the cloud, things are a bit different.

Data engineers suddenly need to think differently and more broadly. Instead of being focused purely on data infrastructure, you are now almost a full-stack engineer (leaving out the final end application, perhaps). Skills are increasingly needed across the broader stack—compute, containers, storage, data movement, performance, network. Here are some design concepts and data stack elements to keep in mind.

Disaggregated Data Stack

Historically, databases were tightly integrated, with all core components built together. Hadoop changed that with colocated computing and storage in a distributed system instead of being in a single or a few boxes. Then the cloud changed that. Today, it is a fully disaggregated stack (*https://oreil.ly/vMQ1r*) with each core element of the database management system being its own layer. Pick each component wisely.

Orchestrate, Orchestrate, Orchestrate

The cloud has created a need for and enabled mass orchestration—whether that's Kubernetes (*https://kubernetes.io*) for containers, Alluxio (*https://www.alluxio.io*) for data, Istio (*https://istio.io*) for APIs, Kafka (*https://oreil.ly/b6T0K*) for events, or Terraform (*https://oreil.ly/ccldM*) for scripting.

Efficiency dramatically increases through abstraction and orchestration. Because a data engineer for the cloud now has full-stack concerns, orchestration can be a data engineer's best-kept secret.

Copying Data Creates Problems

Fundamentally, after data lands in the enterprise, it should not be copied around except, of course, for backup, recovery, and disaster-recovery scenarios. How to make this data accessible to as many business units, data scientists, and analysts as possible with as few new copies created as possible is the data engineer's puzzle to solve. This is where in the legacy DBMS world a buffer pool helped, making sure the compute (query engine) always had access to data stored in a consistent, optimized way in a format that was suitable for the query engine to process, rather than a format optimized for storage. Technologies like Alluxio can dramatically simplify this, bringing data closer to compute and making it more performant and accessible.

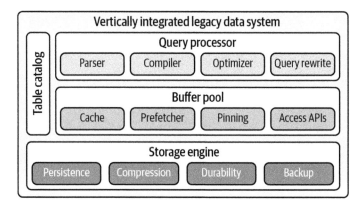

S3 Compatibility

Because of the popularity of Amazon S3, object stores in general will be the next dominant storage systems—at least for a few years (a five- to eight-year cycle, typically). Think ahead and choose a storage tier that will last for some time. S3-compatible object stores should be your primary choice. While they are not great at all data-driven workloads, many technologies help remove their deficiencies.

SQL and Structured Data Are Still In

While SQL has existed since the 1970s, it still is the easiest way for analysts to understand and do something with data. AI models will continue to evolve, but SQL has lasted for close to 50 years. Pick two, or at most three, frameworks to bet on and invest in—but build a platform that will over time support as many as needed. Currently, Presto is turning into a popular SQL query engine choice for the disaggregated stack.

Embrace the Data Lake Architecture

Vinoth Chandar

Oftentimes, data engineers build data pipelines to extract data from external sources, transform it, and enable other parts of the organization to query the resulting datasets. While it's easier in the short term to just build all of this as a single-stage pipeline, a more thoughtful data architecture is needed to scale this model to thousands of datasets spanning multiple tera/petabytes.

Common Pitfalls

Let's understand some common pitfalls with the single-stage approach. First of all, it limits scalability since the input data to such a pipeline is obtained by scanning upstream databases—relational database management systems (RDBMSs) or NoSQL stores—that would ultimately stress these systems and even result in outages. Further, accessing such data directly allows for little standardization across pipelines (e.g., standard timestamp, key fields) and increases the risk of data breakages due to lack of schemas/data contracts. Finally, not all data or columns are available in a single place, to freely cross-correlate them for insights or design machine learning models.

Data Lakes

In recent years, the data lake architecture has grown in popularity. In this model, source data is first extracted with little to no transformation into a first set of raw datasets. The goal of these raw datasets is to effectively model an upstream source system and its data, but in a way that can scale for online analytical processing (OLAP) workloads (e.g., using columnar file formats). All data pipelines that express business-specific transformations are then executed on top of these raw datasets.

Advantages

This approach has several advantages over the single-stage approach, avoiding all the pitfalls listed before:

Scalable design
> Since the data is extracted once from each source system, the additional load on the source system is drastically reduced. Further, extracted data is stored in optimized file formats on petabyte-scale storage systems (e.g., HDFS, cloud stores), which are all specifically optimized for OLAP workloads.

Standardized and schematized
> During the ingestion of the raw datasets, standardization steps can be performed and a schema can be enforced on the data, which validates both structural integrity and semantics. This prevents bad data from ever making its way into the data lake.

Nimble
> Data engineers can develop, test, and deploy changes to transformation business logic independently, with access to large-scale parallel processing using thousands of computing cores.

Unlocks data
> Such a data lake houses all source data together, with rich access to SQL and other tools to explore and derive business insights by joining the data and even producing derived datasets. Machine learning models have unfettered access to all of the data.

Implementation

Here are a few tips for implementing the data lake architecture, based on lessons learned from actually building large data lakes (*https://oreil.ly/cbBGG*):

- Consider ingesting databases in an incremental fashion by using change-capture systems or even approaches based on Java Database Connectivity, or JDBC (e.g., Apache Sqoop), to improve data freshness as well as further reduce load on the databases.

- Standardize event streams from applications and such database change streams into a single event bus (e.g., Apache Kafka, Apache Pulsar).

- Ingest the raw datasets from the event bus by using technologies that can support upserts to compact database changes into a snapshot (e.g., Apache Kudu, Apache Hudi,[1] Apache Hive ACID).

- Design the raw datasets to support efficient retrieval of new records (similar to change capture) by either partitioning your data (e.g., using Apache Hive metastore) or using a system that supports change streams (e.g., Apache Hudi).

---

1 I am part of the PPMC (*https://oreil.ly/DpAUo*) of Apache Hudi, as well as its cocreator.

Embracing Data Silos

Bin Fan and
Amelia Wong

Working in the big data and machine learning space, we frequently hear from data engineers that the biggest obstacle to extracting value from data is being able to access the data efficiently. *Data silos*, isolated islands of data, are often viewed by data engineers as the key culprit. Over the years, many attempts have arisen to resolve the challenges caused by data silos, but those attempts have often resulted in even more data silos. Rather than attempting to eliminate data silos, we believe the right approach is to embrace them.

Why Data Silos Exist

Data silos exist for three main reasons. First, within any organization there is data with varying characteristics (Internet of Things data, behavioral data, transactional data, etc.) that is intended for different uses, and some of that data will be more business-critical than others. This drives the need for disparate storage systems. Second, history has shown that every 5 to 10 years a new wave in storage technologies churns out storage systems that are faster, cheaper, or better designed for certain types of data. Organizations also have a desire to avoid vendor lock-ins and as a result will diversify their data storage. Third, regulations mandate the siloing of data.

Embracing Data Silos

We believe data silos in themselves are not the challenge. The fundamental challenge is how to make data accessible to data engineers without creating more complexity or duplication. Instead of eliminating silos, we propose leveraging a *data orchestration* system, which sits between computing frameworks and storage systems, to resolve data access challenges. We define a data orchestration system as a layer that abstracts data access across storage systems, virtualizes all the data, and presents the data via standardized APIs with a global namespace to data-driven applications.

With a data orchestration system, data engineers can easily access data stored across various storage systems. For example, a data engineer may need to join two tables originally stored in two different regions—a local Hadoop cluster and a remote Hadoop cluster. By implementing a data orchestration system, they can address both locations from a single logical endpoint, simplifying the task of working across disparate systems. Many data orchestration systems (e.g., Alluxio) provide advanced caching capabilities, reducing the performance impact of repeated queries against the source locations. Furthermore, storage teams can make the best storage-purchasing decisions without being shackled by the impact of their decisions on application teams.

Engineering Reproducible Data Science Projects

Dr. Tianhui Michael Li

Just like any scientific field, data science is built on reproducibility. In a reproducible project (*https://oreil.ly/woz2k*), someone else (including the future you) can re-create your results by running a simple command. On the one hand, this means that you should check your analysis code into a source-control tool like Git (*http://www.git.com*). On the other, it also means following DevOps best practices like including dependency lists in machine-readable forms (like *requirements.txt* for pip or *environment.yml* for Conda). You might go one step further and use a Dockerfile. The commands needed to install and run the analysis should also be included. Finally, make sure that you clearly document what to run in a *README.md* file, or preferably in a job runner like Make.

Another important piece of reproducibility is eliminating something we'll call algorithmic randomness from your pipeline in order to maintain consistency. If your data is being subsetted from a larger dataset or your analysis depends on an initial random condition (many of your favorite ones do), you're depending on a random number generator. This can cause the same analysis to yield different results—so make sure your generator is tied to a random seed (*https://oreil.ly/qdHFl*) that's checked into version control. This ensures that your work can be reproduced, and any variation in your results can be attributed to the code or data, not to chance.

If you work in Python, Jupyter notebooks (*https://jupyter.org*) can combine code, visualizations, and explanations in a single document. In the academic world, Nobel Prize winners have used notebooks to demonstrate the existence of gravitational waves (*https://oreil.ly/y5b3c*). In industry, companies like Netflix use notebook templates (*https://oreil.ly/Ojn8E*) to deliver visualizations to stakeholders. Don't be afraid to check notebooks into Git—Netflix does it, and so do we! We restart the kernel and rerun all the analysis from scratch before saving the output, which avoids out-of-order execution mistakes and helps guarantee that we'll get the same results the next time we run it.

Finally, it's always smart to begin a data science project with some idea of how it will be put into production. For instance, designing a pipeline that uses the same data format during the research and production phases will prevent bugs and data corruption issues later. For the same reason, it's also a good idea to sort out how your research code can be put into production before you start, rather than creating separate code for the latter.

When starting off as a data engineer, it's tempting to dive into what you see as the "cutting edge" of the field. But based on our experience, it's a much better investment to focus on the foundations and make sure you can create reproducible, consistent, and production-ready pipelines that are easily accessible to various stakeholders. Though it may not seem as glamorous at first, it will pay dividends over the life of both your project and your career.

Five Best Practices for Stable Data Processing

Christian Lauer

The following five best practices are the basics when it comes to implementing data processes such as ELT or ETL.

Prevent Errors

In case of failure, a rollback should be done—similar to with SQL. If a job aborts with errors, all changes should be rolled back. Otherwise, only $X\%$ of the transaction will be transmitted, and a part will be missing. Finding out what that missing data is will be very hard.

Set Fair Processing Times

How long does a job take to process X data rows? This provides important insights about the process. How often and how long does a process have to run? Which data actuality can I assure my department? What happens when data has to be reloaded?

Use Data-Quality Measurement Jobs

Are my source and target systems compliant? How can I be sure that all data has been transferred? Here, I recommend building up a monitoring strategy. It's always a good idea to measure data quality and to detect errors quickly; otherwise, a lack of trust from the consumer can result.

Ensure Transaction Security

When using database-replication software in your process (for example, AWS Data Migration Service, or DMS) instead of a direct connection between system A and system B, you can run into trouble. I once had a replication job that loaded data from table A and table B at the same time. Both were further processed by an ETL job, but if a dataset from table B was not available because of high latency, and the dataset from table A was processed, the information from table B would be missing. Here, I also recommend adding monitoring, or dispensing of too many additional components in the process.

Consider Dependency on Other Systems

Various circumstances must be taken into account for the source systems:

Availability
> When is a source system available? Consider maintenance cycles and downtimes.

High data load
> The target systems must not receive any unnecessary changes (CDC) from the source system; for example, during peak times. Instead, data transfer could take place in a batch job at night.

Unwanted behavior of other systems
> As described previously, database replication services could ruin your ETL processes, but other problems also can occur; for example, duplicate and inconsistent data. Here, it is important to get to know the source systems and their pitfalls.

Conclusion

For me, these are the five most important building blocks for establishing a stable and secure data process. You should always keep in mind that data quality is important. Otherwise, you might experience a lack of trust from users and business departments.

Focus on Maintainability and Break Up Those ETL Tasks

Chris Moradi

As the data science tent widens, practitioners may excel at using prepared data but lack the skills to do this preparation in a reliable way. These responsibilities can be split across multiple roles and teams, but enormous, productive gains can be achieved by taking a full-stack approach, in which data scientists own the entire process from ideation through deployment.

Whether you're a data scientist building your own ETLs or a data engineer assisting data scientists in this process, making your data pipelines easier to understand, debug, and extend will reduce the support burden for yourself and your teammates. This will facilitate iteration and innovation in the future.

The primary way to make ETLs more maintainable is to follow basic software engineering best practices and break the processing into small and easy-to-understand tasks that can be strung together—preferably with a workflow engine. Small ETL tasks are easier for new contributors and maintainers to understand, they're easier to debug, and they allow for greater code reuse.

Doing too much in a processing step is a common pitfall for both the inexperienced and the highly experienced. With less experience, it can be hard to know how to decompose a large workflow into small, well-defined transformations. If you're relatively new to building ETLs, start by limiting the number of transformations you perform in each task by separating things like joining source tables, creating flag columns, and aggregating the results. You should seek advice and code reviews from those with more experience and the teammates who will help support your ETLs in production. These reviews should focus on simplicity rather than performance.

Highly experienced data engineers can also produce overly dense pipelines because chains of complex transformations feel commonplace. While this is acceptable if they are the only ones maintaining these ETLs, it prohibits less-experienced data scientists or engineers from supporting, modifying, or extending these pipelines. This can block innovation because the data scientists are reliant on a small number of experts to implement changes.

If you're an experienced data engineer, you should consider how easy it is for someone with less experience to understand and build upon your work and think about refactoring so that it's more accessible. Your work doesn't need to be universally understood, but consider how much you and others are gaining from the added complexity.

Breaking pipelines into small tasks may carry computational costs as the work can't be optimized across these boundaries. However, we sometimes focus too much on runtime performance when we should instead focus on the speed of innovation that's enabled. In some cases performance is critical, but optimizing a daily batch job to shave an hour off the runtime may add weeks or even months to the time required to implement future enhancements.

Friends Don't Let Friends Do Dual-Writes

Gunnar Morling

Long gone are the times when enterprise application developers could just put data into their application's database and call it a day. Nowadays, data often needs to be persisted in multiple systems in order to satisfy ever-increasing user requirements: changed data needs to be sent to separate search services, enabling a feature-rich full-text search experience usually not provided by databases themselves, and caches need to be updated, allowing for fast data retrieval without accessing the database itself.

But how can all these data stores—an application's database, a search index, a cache—be kept in sync? We might be tempted to simply issue requests to all these systems for updating the data, but here be dragons.

What if, for instance, the search index temporarily isn't available because of a networking issue? We could think of implementing retry logic, but things quickly get complex there. Worse, even if we *are* able to successfully update all the involved resources, we might end up with data inconsistencies. Unless all the updates are done within a single global transaction (which, in turn, would tie our service quality to the availability of all the resources), we have no ordering guarantees across multiple data changes. If two updates to the same record occur in close temporal proximity, they could be applied in a different order in the search index than in the database. On the surface, things would look good, but the search index would actually provide incorrect results.

And that's why *friends don't let friends do dual-writes*: writes to multiple distributed resources without shared transaction semantics are error prone and will lead to data inconsistencies. But there's hope: if we cannot update multiple resources, we always can update a single one, and that's the application's database. We then can drive the update of the search index, cache, and other secondary systems based on the changes in the database.

This is where change data capture (CDC) comes in: it allows users to react to all the changes in a database and transmit them as events to downstream consumers. This avoids the issues discussed previously: log-based CDC solutions such as Debezium tap into the database transaction log, extracting all data changes in their exact order of transaction serialization.

By propagating change events to consumers through a distributed commit log such as Apache Kafka, the availability concern is also addressed: if a downstream system isn't available for some time, it can simply continue to read change data topics from the point where it left off before. And as the CDC process is asynchronous too, the only synchronously required resource is the database itself.

Another advantage of propagating change events through a distributed commit log is that other consumers and use cases can be enabled by simply rereading change event topics from the beginning. That way, data can be relayed to any other interested service, and all that without relying on dual-writes.

Fundamental Knowledge

Pedro Marcelino

Knowledge is growing exponentially. It is hard to measure the growth of knowledge, especially over a long period of time. However, if we use the number of academic publications as a proxy for knowledge, we can observe that knowledge is doubling every nine years. If you start working today, 20 years from now, when you are in the middle of your career, the amount of knowledge involved in your professional life will be approximately four times more than it is today.

This conclusion would be similar (or even more shocking) if we instead consider the number of books published, the number of scientists, or the amount of data created each day as a proxy for knowledge. And that's scary.

All knowledge workers, such as data engineers, therefore face a challenge. On the one hand, the growth of knowledge leads to an unmanageable need to keep up-to-date with several new concepts, technologies, and frameworks. On the other hand, knowledge is becoming more transient, and what we learn today may be obsolete tomorrow. Since it is hard to believe that in the near future knowledge growth rates will decrease, all data engineers suffer from this particular curse of knowledge.

Thus, the most important question is, how do we deal with this growth of knowledge?

One possible answer is to focus on the fundamentals. In a world of constant change, the fundamentals are more important than ever because they provide a fast track to learning new fields of knowledge as they arise. By definition, *fundamentals* are the primary principles that the rest of the field can be derived from. Thus, if you master the fundamentals, you can master any new emerging field.

Moreover, the fundamentals have stood the test of time. This is a manifestation of the Lindy effect, which states that the future life expectancy of any nonperishable entity is proportional to its current age. Accordingly, we can conclude that, since fundamentals are an intellectual production (a nonperishable entity) that have lasted a long time, they are likely to continue to last much longer.

In a world flooded by an immense amount of knowledge, we need to be able to make sense of information, to distinguish what is important from what is unimportant, and, above all, to combine what we know to fuel our learning and keep up the pace. That requires knowledge. Fundamental knowledge.

Getting the "Structured" Back into SQL

Elias Nema

Not that many questions in computer science have been circulating for nearly 50 years and are still around. How to write SQL is one of them.

Relational databases have dominated the market since the '70s. Then the whole NoSQL movement arose and smoothly evolved into "NewSQL." Recently, all major streaming systems have been adding support for SQL. There must be something really powerful about this language.

With great power comes—you know. SQL is so flexible that it allows you to write queries in almost any form and still get results. The problem is that understanding whether the result makes sense usually requires more effort than producing it. You've seen it yourself, "fixing" joins with a DISTINCT statement or counting rows multiple times.

I argue that most of this can be avoided by writing queries in a structured manner, optimizing for readability first. So how do you make structure? First, begin with the end in mind: what should the answer look like? For example, say you want to analyze revenue for a specific sales channel, categorized by regions. See, it's already a prepared SELECT statement. (In this example, I'm using pseudo-SQL to avoid unrelated details.)

```
SELECT channel, region, SUM(sales)
```

Usually, the main subject would be in the question you are trying to answer. In this example, you want to analyze revenue. So sales is going to be your main entity, the driving table. In FROM, you should always put this table first.

```
FROM sales                    ◄ - - - driving table
```

Now you want to filter for a specific channel. For this, go to the new table, channels. When adding it, think of your query as a tree—the main table is the trunk, and the new table is a branch.

The next step is to group results by region. The sales table has only districts. For regions, you need to go to the districts > cities > regions tables. Here your branch would consist of multiple tables.

The branching metaphor also helps with rules for OUTER joins. Whenever introduced, carry the subject over in all the join conditions until the end of the current branch.

Of course, we looked at quite a simple query here. And SQL is sophisticated nowadays; you can do a variety of window functions and complex aggregations. However, the structure should come first. So, to make your query structured and pleasant to read by following these steps:

1. Begin with the end in mind. Think about what your answer should look like.

2. Find the main subject. Always put this subject into a FROM statement first. If there is more than one subject, wrap each into a common table expression (CTE) and apply these steps to each of them.

3. Add tables to the main one, one intent at a time. For example, the intent might be, "All the following JOINs are here to get the region for a sale."

---

4. Be careful about your joins. Ensure that the table you add has no more than one row per join condition.

5. Move to groupings, analytical functions, and so forth only after you've finished connecting all the data sources.

Once you have learned how to get the data you need from different sources and documented it in the form of a readable structure, the query will tell the story of your analysis by itself. More important, that structure will help others to better understand your intentions and trust your results.

Give Data Products a Frontend with Latent Documentation

Emily Riederer

The rise of DataOps demonstrates the value of bringing DevOps principles to data engineering. Similar, but less explored, is the need to incorporate principles from design and product management into data builds and explicitly craft a good user experience.

Engineers should think critically about building a "frontend" for their data that makes it easy to understand and intuitive to use. For data, specifically, the frontend is not a traditional UI but rather the lump sum of tools and documents that enable users to understand the intent, lineage, and quality of a dataset.

Of course, building this frontend is no small task, and often data engineers are at full capacity with the technical aspects of their work. However, many of the artifacts that data consumers want can be created with little to no incremental effort if engineers embrace latent documentation: systematically documenting their own thought processes and decision making during the engineering process in a way that can be easily shared with and interpreted by users.

The following are examples of latent documentation you can collect for a low-cost data frontend:

Generate a data dictionary while gathering user requirements
    When you talk to users about data requirements (you are talking to users, aren't you?), engage them in the process of documenting these requirements (such as variable names and definitions) in a standardized spreadsheet format. This not only saves potential rework by helping you align with your customers at the start, but also can serve as an excellent start to a data dictionary written in the language of the business.

Utilize a hierarchical variable-naming taxonomy

Variable names are the main way users will interact with your data and one of the most critical components of the user experience. Embrace a hierarchical naming structure that reflects your data model. You might consider a structure like `ENTITY_ATTRIBUTE_DESCRIPTOR_TYPE`; for example, `ACCT_ID`, `ACCT_LOGIN_DT`, `ACCT_LOGIN_DEVICE_CD` for relational data. Taxonomy can both help encode metadata so users interpret field names and intent correctly, and make it easier to program on top of data (e.g., by selecting all fields containing certain common "stubs").

Publicly answer user questions in an FAQ list

Understanding the InnerSource Checklist (*https://oreil.ly/I4FTp*) by Silona Bonewald (O'Reilly) introduces the concept of *passive documentation*: answering user questions in public forums such as Slack or GitHub instead of private channels such as direct messages to create a permanent record. This same strategy can be used to develop an FAQ list for data users.

Depending on your workflow, you might also consider the following:

Visualize the data pipeline

Many popular workflow management systems like Apache Airflow and Prefect visualize your data workflow in a directed acyclic graph. While this type of diagram might be intimidating to an average business user, more-advanced data analysts and data scientists could use it to independently trace data lineage should they ever need to more clearly understand metric definitions or access rawer forms of the data.

Share your expectations and quality checks

Increasingly, engineers are building data-quality checks into their pipelines with tools such as Great Expectations. These tools can not only help validate data and catch errors for downstream users, but also force you to more clearly articulate how you intend the data to behave.

How Data Pipelines Evolve

Chris Heinzmann

In today's world, there is so much data being generated and so much business value waiting to be discovered. How can a data engineer get that data efficiently into the hands of analysts and data scientists?

Enter the data pipeline. Historically, the standard business practice was to set up an ETL pipeline:

Extract
> Take data from a *source* system, usually some sort of scheduler to execute code, called jobs.

Transform
> Modify the data in some way—for example, ensure consistency in naming, provide accurate timestamps, perform basic data cleansing, or calculate baseline metrics.

Load
> Save the data to a *target* system, usually a data warehouse.

The ETL pattern worked well for many years, and continues to work for thousands of companies. If it's not broken, don't fix it. However, traditional ETL can also be intimidating to get started with, and alternatives exist.

For early-stage businesses still navigating product/market fit, forgo the sophisticated pipeline. Questions will be too varied and answers needed too quickly. All that is required is a set of SQL scripts that run as a cron job against the production data at a low-traffic period, and a spreadsheet.

For a company in the middle of a growth stage, setting up an extract, load, transform (ELT) pipeline is appropriate. You will have plenty of unknowns and want to remain as agile as possible in both product and analysis. An ELT pipeline is flexible enough to adapt. Grab the source data with a software-as-a-service (SaaS) provider and/or a few simple SQL scripts and put them in the data warehouse sans transforms as "raw" data. The transforms are done on query or built into the different views.

As the business crystalizes, data starts growing exponentially, and measurements mature, the warehouse will need to codify key metrics and data points in a standard fashion to maintain reliability across your growing organization. Set up this pipeline by modifying the ELT flow with a scheduler *after* the raw data already sits inside a data store. I saw this work well during my time at Grubhub. This leaves you with two data stores, a data lake that serves as a "raw" data store, and a data warehouse containing "transformed" data.

This kind of architecture has the following benefits:

- Data governance becomes easier, as access controls can be different for the raw data and the transformed data.
- The transformations allow for active development and precalculation of important business metrics.
- Each piece in the pipeline is much easier to scale.

Complexity and cost are associated with this architecture, so it makes sense only when the business has achieved some degree of scale.

Pipelines are constructed to get faster insights into the business from data. This is true no matter the scale. The architecture of the pipeline will depend on the scale of the business as well as how well the company has reached product/market fit. It is valuable to know all kinds of architectures as early decisions affect how easy or hard other architectures will be to implement as the business grows.

How to Build Your Data Platform like a Product

Barr Moses and
Atul Gupte

At its core, a *data platform* is a central repository for all data, handling the collection, cleansing, transformation, and application of data to generate business insights. For most organizations, building a data platform is no longer a nice-to-have option but a necessity (*https://oreil.ly/WS9Ph*), with many businesses distinguishing themselves from the competition based on their ability to glean actionable insights from their data.

Much in the same way that many view data itself as a product (*https://oreil.ly/vI48M*), data-first companies like Uber (*https://oreil.ly/MkNEK*), LinkedIn (*https://oreil.ly/cF1PB*), and Facebook (*https://oreil.ly/2w3db*) increasingly view data platforms as products too, with dedicated engineering, product, and operational teams. Despite their ubiquity and popularity, however, data platforms are often spun up with little foresight into who is using them, how they're being used, and what engineers and product managers can do to optimize these experiences.

Whether you're just getting started or are in the process of scaling one, we share three best practices for avoiding these common pitfalls and building the data platform of your dreams.

Align Your Product's Goals with the Goals of the Business

When you're building or scaling your data platform, the first question you should ask is, how does data map to your company's goals?

To answer this question, you have to put on your data-platform product manager hat. Unlike specific product managers, a data-platform product manager (*https://oreil.ly/6mGRU*) must understand the big picture versus area-specific goals. This is because data feeds into the needs of every other functional team (*https://oreil.ly/oNv0K*), from marketing and recruiting to business development and sales.

Gain Feedback and Buy-in from the Right Stakeholders

It goes without saying that receiving buy-in up front and iterative feedback throughout the product development process are both necessary components of the data-platform journey. What isn't as widely understood is whose voices you should care about.

While developing a new data-cataloging system at a leading transportation company, one product manager we spoke with spent *three months* trying to sell the vice president of engineering on her team's idea, only to be shut down in a single email by the VP's chief of staff.

At the end of the day, it's important that this experience nurtures a community of data enthusiasts who build, share, and learn together. Since your platform has the potential to serve the entire company, everyone should feel invested in its success, even if that means making compromises along the way.

Prioritize Long-Term Growth and Sustainability over Short-Term Gains

Data platforms are not successful simply because they benefit from being "first-to-market." For instance, Uber's big data platform (*https://oreil.ly/nN44t*) was built over the course of five years, constantly evolving with the needs of the business, Pinterest (*https://oreil.ly/IbsTa*) has gone through several iterations of its core data analytics product, and LinkedIn has been building and iterating (*https://oreil.ly/NM7oU*) on its data platform since 2008!

Our suggestion: choose solutions that make sense in the context of your organization, and align your plan with these expectations and deadlines. Sometimes, quick wins as part of a larger product development strategy can help with achieving internal buy-in—as long as it's not shortsighted. Rome wasn't built in a day, and neither was your data platform.

Sign Off on Baseline Metrics for Your Data and How You Measure It

It doesn't matter how great your data platform is if you can't trust your data, but *data quality* means different things to different stakeholders. Consequently, your data platform won't be successful if you and your stakeholders aren't aligned on this definition.

To address this, it's important to set baseline expectations for your data reliability (*https://oreil.ly/sF0tF*)—in other words, your organization's ability to deliver high data availability and health throughout the entire data life cycle. Setting clear service-level objectives (SLOs) and service-level indicators (SLIs) for software application reliability is a no-brainer. Data teams should do the same for their data pipelines.

How to Prevent a Data Mutiny

Sean Knapp

Founder and CEO of Ascend

Data teams are on a collision course. We've seen growth in the volume, velocity, and variety of data that leads to more-complex systems, but the most important component of a company's data sophistication is by far the number of people—architects, engineers, analysts, and scientists—able to build new data products, and their efficiency in doing so.

As enterprises scale their efforts and their teams to build new data products, the interconnectedness and resulting complexity can be paralyzing for these groups. Worse still, they often have conflicting priorities, sending them down a path wrought with conflict. For infrastructure teams, building for scale, security, and cost are of the utmost importance, while engineering teams prioritize flexibility, development speed, and maintainability. Meanwhile, data scientists and analysts are focused on availability and discoverability of data, and connectivity of tools.

Catering to just one group's needs is a guaranteed strategy to incite a "data mutiny," in which internal users create shadow IT organizations with a mandate to move quickly and free themselves from the conflicting priorities. However, new processes and technologies can help bring back this balance of speed and flexibility, without risking scale, security, and maintainability.

With DevOps, we enabled more people than ever before to build increasingly complex software products faster and more safely, by introducing modular architectures, declarative configurations, and automated systems. The same is possible with data, meaning we can apply the lessons we've learned from DevOps to save organizations from falling victim to a data mutiny.

Here are some recommendations:

Modular architectures
Today's pipelines all too often resemble a bowl of spaghetti, yet it's essential to have well-defined, modularized pipeline designs. Similar to APIs and microservices, having smaller services that focus on distinct stages enables a data-centric approach to pipeline orchestration and allows for greater flexibility.

Declarative configurations
Similar to what we've seen everywhere, from infrastructure to frontend development, building on a platform that deeply understands how data pipelines work allows us to offload a lot more of that complexity to the underlying engine itself. As a result, the use of declarative systems reduces the implementation complexity and maintenance burden.

Automated systems
Automating many of the manual development steps involved with pipeline creation brings stability, speed, and flexibility to data architectures, regardless of the inevitable changes in data type and applications. Automation lowers the overall design and maintenance costs across the data development life cycle, while improving the quality and reliability of the resulting data pipelines.

Over the past decade, trends have emerged as engineering teams shifted from monolithic to modular, manual to automated, and imperative to declarative—resulting in more-stable foundations for critical components within businesses. These same trends can be leveraged for data teams, providing harmonious balance among otherwise conflicting goals, and helping to prevent data mutinies. In return, data teams gain the benefits of improved productivity, flexibility, and speed to deliver on new, innovative data products.

Know the Value per Byte of Your Data

Dhruba Borthakur

As a data engineer at various data-driven software companies, I observed how new technologies like Hadoop and Amazon S3 enabled product teams to store a lot of data. Compared to earlier systems, these new systems reduced the cost per byte of data so much that it became economically feasible to store terabytes of data without boring a hole in your pocket. It was easy to calculate this metric: divide your total dataset size by its total cost, and you have your *cost-per-byte* metric.

Product engineers started to log every event in their applications, without a second thought: "I'll log fine-grained details about each event, even though I really need only one small piece of this information. It's cheap to log, so why bother to reduce the size of my log record?"

We data engineers were thrilled to flaunt our terabyte sized datasets, compariing our efforts to those of traditional database administrators who typically managed only up to a few hundred gigabytes of data. General Electric's locomotives generate 1TB of data in a single freight route. A Boeing 787 generates half a terabyte per flight. And data engineers help manage this data! This was in the mid-2010s, when enterprises leveraged the rapidly diminishing cost per byte to practically never delete their log data (other than for compliance reasons).

Fast-forward to the early 2020s. Today, I am not challenged by the size of the data that I need to maintain. It is the value that the enterprise extracts from the data that is important to me. What insights are we able to extract from our datasets? Can I use the data when I need it, or do I have to wait for it? These considerations are best captured by a new metric, *value per byte*.

For my enterprise, I have my own way to compute value per byte. If a query touches one specific byte of data, the value of that byte is 1. If a specific byte is not touched by any query, the value of that byte is 0. I compute my value per byte as the percentage of unique bytes that were used to serve any query.

For my multiterabyte dataset, I found that my value per byte is 2.5%. This means that for every 100 bytes of data that I help manage, I am using only the information stored in 2.5 bytes.

What is the value per byte of your enterprise? You might calculate it differently, but if you can increase the value per byte of your system, you can positively impact the data-driven decisions in your enterprise.

Know Your Latencies

Dhruba Borthakur

Every data system has three characteristics that uniquely identify it: the size of the data, the recency of the data, and the latency of queries on that data. You are probably familiar with the first one, but the other two are sometimes an afterthought.

As a data engineer, I have frequently deployed a big data system for one use case. Then a new user uses the same data system for a different use case and complains, "Oh, my query latencies are slower than my acceptable limit of 500 milliseconds" or "My query is not finding data records that were produced in the most recent 10 seconds."

At the very outset of engineering a data system, the three things that I ask myself are as follows:

What is my data latency?

The data latency can vary widely. An annual budgeting system would be satisfied if it had access to all of last month's data and earlier. Similarly, a daily reporting system will probably be happy if it can get access to the most recent 24 hours of data. An online software-gaming leaderboard application would be satisfied with analyzing data that is produced in the most recent 1 second and earlier.

What is my query latency?

If I am building a daily reporting system, I can afford to build a system that is optimized for overall throughput. The latency of a query could take a few minutes or even a few hours, because I need to produce a set of reports only once every day. On the other hand, a backend application that powers personalized news stories for a reader would typically demand latencies of a few milliseconds, and this data system would need to be engineered to optimize query latency.

What are my queries per second?

If my data system is powering an application on a mobile device, my queries per second (QPS) would likely be tens or hundreds of concurrent queries. If my data system is used to build a daily reporting system, it will need to support 5 to 10 concurrent queries at most.

The answers to these three questions determine the type of data system you should use. Data latency is dominated by data pipelines, also called extract, transform, load (ETL) processes. You can use an ETL process to weed out records with bad data or to pregenerate aggregates over time ranges. The ETL process adds latencies to your data, and a shorter pipeline means that you get to query your most recent data.

Query latency and QPS are dominated by the database that serves your queries. If you use a key/value store, you will get very low query latencies but will have to implement a larger part of your business logic in your application code. Alternatively, if you use a data warehouse that exposes a SQL API, you can delegate a larger share of your application logic via SQL to the data warehouse, but the latency of your queries will be higher than with a key/value store and you will be limited to 5 or 10 concurrent queries.

Learn to Use a NoSQL Database, but Not like an RDBMS

Kirk Kirkconnell

It keeps happening: I keep reading posts or talking to people who are having problems with NoSQL databases, and so many times they blame the tool. NoSQL databases may no longer be the new kid on the block, but many people still seem to misunderstand when and why to use them.

I am speaking primarily of data modeling with NoSQL databases, especially when it comes to JSON document, wide column, and key/value types of databases. Some people still try to use them just as they did an RDBMS, but perhaps worse. They create a schema in the NoSQL database that is like a relational schema, and then perform what I would call a "naive migration" or "naive database schema." Then they use it as a dumping ground for data, hoping to make sense of it by using a query language to work through the data. At that point, they wonder why the NoSQL database does not perform or scale well, or gets too expensive.

If you are performing these naive actions, you, too, are most likely failing to understand what these NoSQL databases are optimized for, the trade-offs you are making, the power they bring to the party, and how best to model data for easy access.

NoSQL databases perform and scale best when your schema is designed to model the application's access patterns, the frequency with which those patterns are called, and the velocity of access. The goal should be to precompute the answers to these access patterns, and only rarely ask questions of the data (ad hoc querying). This is true whether the data is key/value, wide column, or JSON document store.

Can you ask questions in NoSQL databases? Sure, but that is not where most of them shine. You take a hit on performance, scalability, cost, or a mix of those. The more you try to use a NoSQL database as a general-purpose database, the more you get into the "jack of all trades, master of none" arena that RDBMSs have unfortunately been shoehorned into. For best performance, scalability, and cost, asking questions of your data should be the minority of the requests in OLTP-type NoSQL databases.

I propose a seemingly simple task the next time you think about creating a new application with a NoSQL database or migrating from an RDBMS to a NoSQL database. First, document all of that workload's access patterns. What exact data is needed, when, and at what velocity? This should guide you as you create a schema. This schema may be more complex on the surface, but the application can assemble the ID/primary key/partition key so it is not asking questions, but just getting the data efficiently. Next, figure out what questions you need to satisfy with a query. You need to have the right balance of quick and cheap data access for most things, and using queries only when you really need them.

If you cannot do these tasks, including documenting all of the application's access patterns ahead of time, a NoSQL database may not be the correct solution for your workload. You might be better off with an RDBMS that allows more flexibility at the expense of scalability.

Let the Robots Enforce the Rules

Anthony Burdi

Dealing with messy inputs is part of our job as data professionals. We don't always have to be pedantic (*https://oreil.ly/WUars*), but asking data producers to structure their inputs in a certain way eases our burden with this not-so-glamorous work.

Great! Now our incoming data is cleaner. But then we realize that our burden just shifted to an interpersonal one: "asking" others to follow specific rules, read docs, and follow processes. For some of us, this is emotionally demanding and may end up making our jobs more difficult than if we just dealt with the messy data ourselves.

What do we do about it? The same thing we do with every other boring, repetitive, nitpicky, definable task: Pinky, (*https://oreil.ly/jrDmm*) automate it (*https://xkcd.com/1319*)!

Here are a few validation-robot job description ideas:

- Use a Google form to capture data or visualization requests and simultaneously ask key questions—for example, what is the problem, why are you requesting it, what is the deliverable, the priority, etc. (See also Sam Bail's wonderful blog post "Just One More Stratification!" (*https://oreil.ly/msshg*).)

  Key bonus: Since the robot already asked your standard set of questions, you can start the conversation with the requester wielding some context, or even skip it altogether. Use a drop-down list (yay, validation!) rather than free-form text entry where possible.

  Double bonus: You can track the types of requests coming in so you can inform the planning and build-out of self-service tools.

Extra points: Email new requests to your project-tracking software (Jira, Asana, etc.) for automatic inclusion into an "incoming request" backlog to be groomed and prioritized.

- Add a CODEOWNERS file (*https://oreil.ly/hUNfU*) to a repository, defining the data schema or form validation. For example, you may be capturing user profile information in a Django site that will later be used in a cohort analysis. Add a CODEOWNERS entry to ensure someone from the analytics team reviews any changes to the model definitions or form validations.

  Key bonus: While it is good practice to loop in analytics team members early for any proposed data model design changes, this ensures that at least they have the chance to review and prepare for changes before they are shipped.

- Add a moat around your analytics pipeline by adding data validation on ingestion. Using a tool like Great Expectations (*https://oreil.ly/RvdgL*), you can validate the incoming data before it is loaded into the rest of your processing pipeline; for example, as a preprocessing step in your pipeline or when users upload files by using an upload tool like that used at Heineken (*https://oreil.ly/KBIvB*).

  Key bonus: Even informed, well-intentioned people make mistakes. This ensures issues are caught early and without distracting other team members or affecting downstream products.

  Double bonus: The analytics team can define what correct data should look like by writing Expectations, and use data docs to share the definition of "correct."

In short, adding validation everywhere that you can (within reason!) yields two clear benefits: you get cleaner data, and the computer can be the bad guy. Save your emotional reserves for more important conversations.

Listen to Your Users—but Not Too Much

Amanda Tomlinson

We've all seen the cool infographics, but no one needs to tell a data engineer about the immense and ever-increasing amount of data being generated every day. We're all living it.

We're extracting it, transforming it, landing it (now considering whether we should maybe have started landing before transforming), cleaning it (what, you're saying we should stop cleaning it?), deciding where and for how long to store it, standing up new infrastructure to handle the sheer volume of it, filtering it, joining it, building KPIs and models from it, creating workflows for it, exposing it, cataloging it, monitoring it (easy enough when we started, but increasingly difficult a few years in). With so much to do and so much demand from our stakeholders, it's not at all surprising that so many data teams, especially those serving internal customers, get so caught up in the technical aspects of data engineering that they forget to consider who their users are and what they actually need. Data is data, right?

Before too long, this will lead to frustration, wasted effort, and a lack of confidence in the data team. Yep, all of the stuff I've listed is hugely important, but it's just as important to realize that not all of your users are the same, and to take a step back and consider what they need from the data you produce and what they need from you.

But you shouldn't cater to their every demand. A certain level of satisfaction comes from delivering requirements and closing tickets, but simply churning out solutions creates long-term problems. A fine balance needs to be struck between delivering what your users need and maintaining a sustainable, scalable data function.

For me, this starts with a vision and strategy for the engineering team. If that seems too ambitious, at the very least set some design principles or guardrails. Next, start treating the demands received by your team as nothing more than conversation starters. These are simply insights into what your customers want from you, not fully formed requirements.

To turn them into requirements, you need to dig a bit deeper to understand the problems your customers are trying to solve with your data. Create personas to allow you to understand the various data users and use cases within your organization; look for the commonalities and apply your design principles to allow you to produce data products to serve these. Take ownership of your data and become the expert in serving it up to your users in the right way.

Low-Cost Sensors and the Quality of Data

Dr. Shivanand Prabhoolall Guness

In 2016, I was working on a project witht the aim of developing inexpensive air quality monitoring products using low-cost sensors and low-power devices such as Raspberry Pis and Arduinos. So, to begin the project, we ordered sensors and boards to do a proof of concept.

Our first issue was with the low-cost sensors. We ordered only the required number of sensors: one particulate matter sensor, one nitrogen oxide sensor, and one ozone sensor for one board. The plan was to set up a couple of monitoring sensors around a site and monitor the air quality for one year. We set up redundancies to protect the data in case the internet was not working, by storing the data on an SD card. After the first couple of weeks of testing, we had a power surge and lost all the data on the SD card. The Raspberry Pi was damaged, but the sensors were reused, as they seemed to be working.

The second issue was with the internet. As I said, when it stopped working at the site, all the data was being stored on the SD card. This happened multiple times during our data-capture phase. We reordered the sensors and boards that were damaged, but they took a long time to be delivered, which in turn affected the amount of data we were able to capture. After the initial phase, we also realized that the sensors used during the power surge had been damaged and were giving erroneous output.

We learned the following lessons from this project:

- Always buy redundant materials, especially those that cannot be sourced locally.
- Have redundancy for all essential aspects of the project, such as power and internet.
- Never reuse sensors that have been in a power-related incident.
- Keep an eye on the quality of the data from the very first day.

The project was a great learning experience, but we had to learn the hard way. In hindsight, if I had to redo this project, I would have run the sensing modules on batteries to avoid power-related issues, bought better-quality sensors to get better-quality results, and had a redundant system to collect all the data from the different sensors locally, instead of storing it on each and every sensor.

Another potential idea, as the data was already going to the cloud for processing and deploying on a dashboard, would have been to add an abnormality-detection mechanism to inform us of any potential malfunction in the sensors. Because of the problems we encountered, the usable data from our one year of collection was reduced to a period of five months.

Maintain Your Mechanical Sympathy

Tobias Macey

As a new technologist, you have an endless variety of lessons to learn—everything from the fundamentals of logic, through syntax and software design, and on to building and integrating large distributed systems. After years of practice, ceaseless learning, and inscrutable errors, you will internalize an understanding of more computational errata than you could possibly foresee. In this torrent of information, your perpetual bafflement will be washed away, along with your *beginner's mind* (*https://oreil.ly/brevD*).

One thing that will serve you well on every step of your journey is a healthy dose of mechanical sympathy (*https://oreil.ly/B4AQQ*). It is possible to write useful software, build data platforms, or produce valuable analytics without ever understanding all of the underlying infrastructure and computation. However, when something breaks or you run into confusing performance issues, that understanding will prove invaluable.

Regardless of your chosen specialization, whether it is data engineering, data science, web development, or any other of an infinite gradation, you will be navigating an endless sea of abstractions. Each layer of indirection brings you further from the hardware that is diligently churning through your demanding instructions and winging your data across the world at light speed.

By considering the physical implementations of how CPUs execute instructions, the way that memory registers are populated and accessed, and the complex dance of network connections, you will gain a greater appreciation for what is possible, what is practical, and when you might want to take a different approach. It is not necessary (nor is it feasible) to become an expert in all of the systems and software that power your specific project. Instead, you should aim to learn just enough about them to understand their limitations and to know what you don't know.

For data engineers, some of the foundational principles that will prove most useful are the different access speeds for networked services, hard drives of various types, and system memory. All of these contribute greatly to the concept of data gravity (*https://oreil.ly/BXEun*), which will influence your decisions about how and when to move information between systems, or when to leave it in place and bring your computation to the data. It is also helpful to know the difference between computational architectures, such as general-purpose CPUs (*https://oreil.ly/a14qQ*) versus GPUs (*https://oreil.ly/PcOiJ*) versus ASICs (*https://oreil.ly/nXtV2*), and when to leverage each of their capabilities.

At the end of the day, there is always a shiny new tool, or language, or problem, but you will always be well served by the time that you invest in understanding the fundamental principles underlying everything that we do as software professionals.

Metadata ≥ Data

Jonathan Seidman

My first real experience in the big data world was helping to deploy Apache Hadoop clusters at Orbitz Worldwide, a heavily trafficked online travel site.[1] One of the first things we did was deploy Apache Hive on our clusters and provide access to our developers to start building applications and analyses on top of this infrastructure.

This was all great, in that it allowed us to unlock tons of value from all of this data we were collecting. After a while, though, we noticed that we ended up with numerous Hive tables that basically represented the same entities. From a resource standpoint, this wasn't that awful, since even in the dark ages of the aughts, storage was pretty cheap. However, our users' time was not cheap, so all the time they spent creating new Hive tables, or searching our existing tables to find the data they needed, was time they weren't spending on getting insights from the data.

The lesson we learned at Orbitz was that it's a mistake to leave data management planning as an afterthought. Instead, it's best to start planning your data management strategy early, ideally in parallel with any new data initiative or project.

Having a data management infrastructure that includes things like metadata management isn't only critical for allowing users to perform data discovery and make optimal use of your data. It's also crucial for things like complying with existing and new government regulations around data. It's difficult, for example, to comply with a customer's request to delete their data if you don't know what data you actually have and where it is.

While it's probably relatively straightforward to identify datasets to capture metadata for, and define what that metadata should contain, the bigger challenge can be putting in place processes and tools to capture the metadata and make it available. The fact is, you don't have to find the perfect tool to

---

1 Thanks to Ted Malaska for some of the ideas that motivated this chapter.

manage all of your data, and it's possible that no single tool will allow you to effectively manage your data across all your systems. This is definitely a case where even a nonoptimal solution will put you far ahead of having no solution in place.

Whether you use vendor-provided tools, third-party tools, or even decide to roll your own (*https://oreil.ly/upPTs*), the important thing is to have a process and plan in place early, and ensure that you carry that process throughout your data projects.

Metadata Services as a Core Component of the Data Platform

Lohit VijayaRenu

An explosion of unstructured data has introduced new challenges around data discovery, data management, and security for organizations. As the amount of data and the complexity of its usage has increased, considering a unified metadata services as part of your data platform has become even more important. Today, both structured and unstructured data together provide crucial information to derive meaningful business insights. Data engineers should look for the following features in any metadata services they are considering for their organization: discoverability, security control, schema management, and an application interface and service guarantee.

Discoverability

The most obvious and common usage of a metadata service is to provide an interface for users to discover data and its partitions. If a data platform has various storage systems, having a common interface for discovering any dataset will help users build generic solutions. Users should have a well-defined interface for querying the dataset and its partitions, which can be translated to an actual physical location by the metadata service. User applications need not hardcode data locations anymore; instead, they can be exposed to interfaces that can help them discover existing and updated data in different storage systems.

Security Control

With unified location management, a rich set of security controls can be enforced across the organization. The metadata service should be able to handle authorization rules for the same data across different storage systems. Interfaces to define, update, and enforce security policies should be exposed. The metadata service should act as a data guardian to make sure that policies are never violated. A good metadata service should also have strong auditing features.

Schema Management

The metadata service should provide features for defining and querying the schema associated with the data it manages. A rich schema enables users to build efficient applications. It also provides insights for security enforcers to fine-tune access control and authorization rules on a dataset based on the data content. A good metadata service should also provide schema validation and versioning features.

Application Interface and Service Guarantee

Being a critical component, the service should be built and supported to be highly available. The application interface should be easy to use and well defined in order to connect with various libraries and systems. The metadata service should be able to support evolving data models and applications.

While no single system may provide all these features, data engineers should consider these requirements while choosing one or more services to build their metadata service. Many large organizations are either evolving their existing services or using open source software to support these features.

Mind the Gap: Your Data Lake Provides No ACID Guarantees

Einat Orr

The modern data lake architecture is based on object storage as the lake, utilizing streaming and replication technologies to pour the data into the lake, and a rich ecosystem of applications that consume data directly from the lake, or use the lake as their deep storage. This architecture is cost-effective and allows high throughput when ingesting or consuming data.

So why is it still extremely challenging to work with data? Here are some reasons:

- We're missing isolation. The only way to ensure isolation is by using permissions or copying the data. Using permissions reduces our ability to maximize our data's value by allowing access to anyone who may benefit from the data. Copying is not manageable, as you can then lose track of what is where in your lake.

- We have no atomicity—in other words, we can't rely on transactions to be performed safely. For example, there is no native way to guarantee that no one will start reading a collection before it has finished writing.

- We can't ensure cross-collection consistency (and in some cases, consistency even for a single collection). Denormalizing data in a data lake is common; for example, for performance considerations. In such cases, we may write the same data in two formats, or index it differently, to optimize for two different applications or two different use cases. (Note that this is required since object storage has poor support of secondary indices.) If one of those processes fails while the other succeeds, you get an inconsistent lake, and you risk providing the data consumers an inconsistent view of the world.

- We have no reproducibility. There is no guarantee that operations involving data + code are reproducible, as data identified in a certain way may change without changing its identity: we can replace an object with an object of the same name, but containing different content.

- We have low manageability. The lineage between datasets and the associations to the code that created them are managed manually or by human-defined and human-configured naming standards.

How do we work around these limitations? First and foremost, we must know not to expect those guarantees. Once you know what you are in for, you will make sure to put in place the guarantees you need, depending on your requirements and contracts you have with your customers who consume data from the data lake.

In addition, centralized metastores such as the Hive metastore can alleviate the pain of a lack of atomicity and consistency across collections, and versioned data formats such as Hudi can ease the strain of isolation and separation of readers from writers. Frameworks like lakeFS can provide a safe data lake management environment with guarantees of atomicity, consistency, isolation, and durability (ACID), while supporting the use of Hive and Hudi.

Modern Metadata for the Modern Data Stack

Prukalpa Sankar

The data world recently converged around the best set of tools for dealing with massive amounts of data, aka the *modern data stack*. The good? It's super fast, easy to scale up in seconds, and requires little overhead. The bad? It's still a noob at bringing governance, trust, and context to data.

That's where metadata comes in. In the past year, I've spoken to more than 350 data leaders to understand their challenges with traditional solutions and construct a vision for modern metadata in the modern data stack. The four characteristics of modern metadata solutions are introduced here.

Data Assets > Tables

Traditional data catalogs were built on the premise that tables were the only asset that needed to be managed. That's completely different now.

BI dashboards, code snippets, SQL queries, models, features, and Jupyter notebooks are all data assets today. The new generation of metadata management needs to be flexible enough to intelligently store and link different types of data assets in one place.

Complete Data Visibility, Not Piecemeal Solutions

Earlier data catalogs made significant strides in improving data discovery. However, they didn't give organizations a single source of truth.

Information about data assets is usually spread across different places—data-lineage tools, data-quality tools, data-prep tools, and more. Modern metadata solutions should help teams finally achieve the holy grail, a single source of information for every data asset.

Built for Metadata That Itself Is Big Data

We're fast approaching a world in which metadata itself is big data. Processing metadata will help teams understand and trust their data better. The fundamental elasticity of the cloud makes this possible like never before. For example, by parsing through SQL query logs, it's possible to automatically create column-level lineage, assign a popularity score to every data asset, and deduce the potential owners and experts for each asset.

Embedded Collaboration at Its Heart

A few years ago, data was primarily consumed by the IT team. Today, data teams are more diverse than ever—data scientists and engineers, business analysts, product managers, and more. Each of these people has their own favorite and diverse data tools, everything from Jupyter to SQL.

Because of the fundamental diversity in modern data teams, modern metadata solutions need to integrate seamlessly with teams' daily workflows. This is where the idea of embedded collaboration comes alive.

Embedded collaboration is about work happening where you are, with the least amount of friction—like requesting access to data when you get a link, for example, in Google Docs, which the owner can approve from Slack. This can unify dozens of micro-workflows that waste time, frustrate, and fatigue data teams.

We're at an inflection point in metadata management—a shift from slow, on-premises solutions to a new era, built on the principles of embedded collaboration common in modern tools. While we don't know everything about the future of data catalogs, it's clear that we're about to see modern metadata take its rightful place in the modern data stack.

Most Data Problems Are Not Big Data Problems

Thomas Nield

When the *big data* buzzword peaked in 2015, I remember NoSQL, Hadoop, MongoDB, and other unstructured data technologies being touted as the future of analytics. Many organizations started collecting data faster than they could organize and store it, so they simply dumped it on a cluster and scaled horizontally as needed. Many companies put enormous expense into migrating off relational databases like MySQL and onto big data platforms like Apache Hadoop.

Amidst this movement, I was teaching an O'Reilly online training on SQL. I had one participant suggest that relational databases and SQL might be legacy technology. If the lack of horizontal scaling was not enough reason, relational databases have all this pesky overhead to structure data in a normalized fashion, as well as to enforce data validation and primary/foreign keys. The internet and connectivity of devices caused an explosion of data, so scalability became the selling point of NoSQL and big data.

The irony is that SQL interfaces were added to these big data platforms, and this happened for a reason. Analysts found NoSQL languages difficult and wanted to analyze data in a relational data fashion. A great majority of data problems are best modeled as relational database structures. An ORDER has a CUSTOMER and a PRODUCT associated with it. It just makes sense that these pieces of information should be normalized in separate tables rather than as a blob of JSON. Even better, there's peace of mind knowing the database software will validate an ORDER and check that the CUSTOMER and PRODUCT do, in fact, exist, rather than let data corruption quietly creep in because of bugs on the frontend.

The truth is, most data problems are not big data problems. Anecdotally, 99.9% of problems I've encountered are best solved with a traditional relational database.

Valid cases for using NoSQL platforms definitely exist, especially when an enormous amount of unstructured data has to be stored (think social media posts, news articles, and web scrapes). But with operational data, relational databases force you to think carefully about how your data model works and to get it right the first time. Operational data of this nature rarely gets so large that a relational database cannot be scaled.

I will leave you with the following table to help aid your SQL-versus-NoSQL decisions.

Feature	SQL	NoSQL	Winner
Integrity/ consistency	Data is enforced with logical relationships, minimized redundancy, and "up-to-date" consistency.	Simple key/value and document storage does not enforce any rules or structure. Redundancy and write latency are common.	SQL
Design changes	Easy to "add" to a database, but harder to modify one.	NoSQL can quickly and arbitrarily change what data it stores.	NoSQL
Analysis	SQL is a universal language that makes accessing and analyzing data simple.	SQL support is sparse, and proprietary languages are esoteric and hardly universal.	SQL
Programming	Programmers of Java, Python, and .NET have to map entities to tables, which can be tedious. But data integrity is a given.	Programming against a NoSQL database is quick and simple, but the onus is on the programmer to validate data.	*Draw*
Performance	Relational databases can store data for most use cases, but struggle with true "big data" cases. Integrity constraints also slow down performance.	NoSQL is capable of storing vast amounts of data with horizontal scaling. It also performs quickly due to horizontal scaling and no integrity constraints.	NoSQL

Moving from Software Engineering to Data Engineering

John Salinas

The move from software engineering to data engineering is rewarding and exciting. Data engineering is everything software engineering is: passion and principles for solving technical challenges efficiently and elegantly. But you expand your craft to include analytical and data-related problems. This involves solving problems at an even larger scale, and also helping people find insights from the problems you are solving.

When I first started in data engineering, I felt lost because there was so much to learn. But like you, I love learning. I was thrilled by the challenge to learn new technologies and new patterns. It's been comforting to realize that all the same principles still apply—things like using abstraction, keeping things simple, and building applications so they are scalable and easy to maintain. Also, all my experience is still relevant, and even more important, so are skills like troubleshooting, scaling enterprise applications, API development, networking, programming, and scripting.

With data engineering, you solve problems similar to those in software engineering, but at a larger scale. I've worked on code that processes billions of events. I wore it as a badge of honor that traditional technologies and platforms would break with the amount of information we were trying to process. Early on, we broke our relational database; when we tried to replicate the data to another database, the replication process could not keep up. Also, one time in our Hadoop environment, we lost over 170TB of data. Don't worry; we were able to recover it, but I was shocked at how much data our project was processing.

And it's not just technology that you break; you also end up breaking mindsets. As a developer, you are comfortable with arrays, structs, objects, enums, and JSON format, but when you introduce these concepts to analysts familiar with only tabular data and primitive data types, it creates an opportunity to teach them about these new things.

With all of these challenges, you have to rethink traditional approaches and get creative when solving problems. Your day-to-day challenges grow from operational use cases to including analytical use cases too. The infrastructure you create not only has to support real-time production traffic that could be customer-facing but also provide insights to analysts looking for patterns in the massive amounts of data in your application. It's an engineering challenge to support both at the same time.

Moving to data engineering provides many exciting benefits. It allows you to learn new things. It allows you to mentor folks based on your experience. And it allows you to solve unique and large problems.

Observability for Data Engineers

Barr Moses

As companies become increasingly data driven, the technologies underlying the rich insights data provides have grown more nuanced and complex. Our ability to collect, store, aggregate, and visualize this data has largely kept up with the needs of modern data teams (think domain-oriented data meshes (*https://oreil.ly/O5FHd*), cloud warehouses (*https://oreil.ly/ONHyN*), and data-modeling solutions (*https://oreil.ly/AdGhC*)), but the mechanics behind data quality (*https://oreil.ly/5w7ra*) and integrity have lagged.

How Good Data Turns Bad

After speaking with several hundred data-engineering teams, I've noticed three primary reasons for good data turning bad:

More and more data sources
> Nowadays, companies use anywhere from dozens to hundreds of internal and external data sources to produce analytics and ML models. Any one of these sources can change in unexpected ways and without notice, compromising the data the company uses to make decisions.

Increasingly complex data pipelines
> Data pipelines are increasingly complex, with multiple stages of processing and nontrivial dependencies among various data assets. With little visibility into these dependencies, any change made to one dataset can impact the correctness of dependent data assets.

Bigger, more specialized data teams
> Companies are increasingly hiring more and more data analysts, scientists, and engineers to build and maintain the data pipelines, analytics, and ML models that power their services and products. Miscommunication is inevitable and will cause these complex systems to break as changes are made.

Introducing Data Observability

The good news? Data engineering is going through its own renaissance, and we owe a big thank you to our counterparts in DevOps (*https://oreil.ly/ CsI15*).

For the past decade or so, software engineers have leveraged targeted solutions to ensure high application uptime while keeping downtime to a minimum. In data, we call this phenomenon data downtime (*https://oreil.ly/ avdLm*). This refers to periods of time when data is partial, erroneous, missing, or otherwise inaccurate, and it only multiplies as data systems become increasingly complex.

By applying the same principles of software application observability and reliability (*https://oreil.ly/BemdH*) to data, these issues can be identified, resolved, and even prevented, giving data teams confidence in their data so they can deliver valuable insights. Data observability has five pillars.[1]

 DATA OBSERVABILITY PILLARS

Freshness | Distribution | Volume | Schema | Lineage

Each pillar encapsulates a series of questions that, in aggregate, provide a holistic view of data health:

Freshness
Is the data recent? When was the last time it was generated? What upstream data is included/omitted?

Distribution
Is the data within accepted ranges? Is it properly formatted? Is it complete?

Volume
Has all the data arrived?

Schema
How has the schema changed? Who has made these changes, and for what reasons?

---

1 Image courtesy of Monte Carlo.

Lineage

What are the upstream and downstream assets impacted by a given data asset? Who are the people generating this data, and who is relying on it for decision making?

As data leaders increasingly invest in data-reliability solutions that leverage data observability, I anticipate that this field will continue to intersect with other major trends in data engineering, including data meshes, machine learning, cloud data architectures, and the delivery of data products as platforms (*https://oreil.ly/zH7i8*).

Perfect Is the Enemy of Good

Bob Haffner

"Le mieux est l'ennemi du bien," loosely translated as "Perfect is the enemy of good," is a saying that most attribute to Voltaire. It's a cautionary phrase about the perceived value of chasing perfection versus the reality of it. This phrase can apply to numerous domains, including data engineering.

Suggesting that perfection is not the goal often invites skepticism from data engineers. After all, developing data products requires precision and a detail-oriented approach. Further, most data engineers have been a part of rushed implementations only to have it come back to haunt them. Sprinkle in a natural aversion to risk, and there are multiple reasons people would challenge the notion that stopping short of perfection is a good idea.

However, this is not a plea for shortcuts. Instead, I'm advocating for delivering faster and implementing only the valuable features.

This concept of delivering faster is similar to Agile's principle of shipping a minimum viable product (MVP). The value of quickly putting a product in the hands of a user cannot be overstated. For example, if your leaders require three metrics to run the business and you have only one completed, ship it. Driving the organization with some insight is always better than driving with none.

The only thing that might be worse than waiting to ship a viable product is developing the remaining features in the pursuit of perfection. These remaining features can often take longer to implement than others or provide less value, or both. For example, if adding a dashboard visualization for a single user requires breaking model and pipeline changes, the payoff probably does not warrant the effort. All of a solution's proposed features should be scrutinized for their projected return on investment, but be particularly vigilant about ones at the bottom of the priority list.

Data engineering is a challenging endeavor that is often fraught with complexity. By delivering faster and implementing only the valuable features, you can reduce the risk and increase your chances of success.

Pipe Dreams

Scott Haines

Senior principal software engineer/software architect

One subtle and novel paradigm in computer systems architecture is the concept of *message passing*. This simple, albeit useful construct allowed for an order of magnitude of gains in parallel processing by allowing processes (applications, kernel tasks, etc.) within a single computer OS to take part in a conversation. The beauty of this was that processes could now participate in conversations in either synchronous or asynchronous fashion and distribute work among many applications without the necessary overhead of locking and synchronization.

This novel approach to solving parallel processing tasks within a single system was further expanded to distributed systems processing with the advent of the *message queue as a service*. The basic message queue allowed for one or many channels (or topics) to be created in a distributed first-in, first-out (FIFO) style of queue that could be run as a service on top of a network-addressable location (e.g., *ip-address:port*). Now many systems across many servers could communicate in a distributed, shared work style, a decomposition of tasks.

It isn't hard to conceptualize how the *pipeline architecture* grew out of the concept of distributed systems communicating over network-addressable message queues. It kind of makes sense on a macro level. Essentially, we had all of the components of the modern pipeline architecture sitting on the assembly line, just waiting to be assembled. But first we had to solve a tiny little issue: failure in the face of partially processed messages.

As you may imagine, if we have a distributed queue and take a message from that queue, we can assume that the queue will purge said message, and life will go on. However, in the face of failure—no matter where you point the blame—if the message is purged before the work is done, that will result in data loss with no means of recovery. Now this is where things evolved.

Given that we wanted to ensure that our applications would complete all work they took from the queue, it made sense to store a log of the messages within a channel (or topic), and allow our systems to keep track of what they consumed and essentially where their processing left off. This simple idea of acknowledging where an application was in the queue led to the concept of *offset tracking* and *checkpointing* for a consumer group within a queue.

Apache Kafka was the first project that treated a message queue as a reliable and, more importantly, replay-able queue that could easily be divided and shared among multiple applications within a shared consumer group. Now there was a reliable, highly available, and highly scalable system that could be used for more than just message passing, and this essentially created the foundation of the streaming pipeline architecture.

Preventing the Data Lake Abyss

Scott Haines

Senior principal software engineer/software architect

Everyone has worked under the wrong assumptions at one point or another in their careers, and in no place have I found this more apparent than when it comes to legacy data and a lot of what ends up in most companies' data lakes.

The concept of the data lake evolved from the more traditional data warehouse, which was originally envisioned as a means to alleviate the issue of data silos and fragmentation within an organization. The data warehouse achieved this by providing a central store where *all data can be accessed*, usually through a traditional SQL interface or other business intelligence tools. The data lake takes this concept one step further and allows you to dump *all of your data in its raw format (unstructured or structured)* into a horizontally scalable massive data store (HDFS/S3) where it can be stored almost indefinitely.

Over the course of many years, what usually starts with the best of intentions can easily turn into a black hole for your company's most valuable asset as underlying data formats change and render older data unusable. This problem seems to arise from three central issues:

- A basic lack of ownership for the team producing a given dataset
- A general lack of good etiquette or data hygiene when it comes to preserving backward compatibility with respect to legacy data structures
- Starting off on the wrong foot when creating a new dataset, with no support from other data-modeling or data-engineering experts

I have found that a simple approach to solving these data-consistency issues come from establishing what I call *data contracts*.

Establishing Data Contracts

The ever-growing need for quality data within an organization almost demands the establishment of data contracts ahead of time. This means taking things further than just adhering to and providing a schema for your data, to also generating a plan for or story about what fields exist when, where, and why.

This contract is your data's API and should be updated and versioned with any change in your producing code. Knowing when a field will exist (or not) saves people time and reduces frustration.

From Generic Data Lake to Data Structure Store

Taking this idea to the next level requires the producing team to have *compiled libraries* for both producing and consuming their data. These libraries should also provide unit tests to ensure full backward compatibility across changes to the underlying data structures. Two commonly used data structure frameworks are Apache Avro and Google Protocol Buffers. Both allow you to define your data schemas in a platform-agnostic way and ultimately give you the type safety you'll never have with traditional JSON.

These versioned and compiled libraries help ensure that each byte of data stored adheres to strict validation and is accountable to the version of the data contract. This establishes a simple rule that each record will be preserved in a versioned format that will be at the very least backward compatible and in a format that can easily be extracted and used for years to come.

This up-front effort will lead to productivity across all data-consuming entities in your company. Instead of road maps being derailed with long periods of *let's play find the missing data* (or literally jettisoning or draining the lake to start over because of a general lack of trust in the data's integrity), you can get back to having a data lake that is an invaluable shared resource used for any of your data needs: from analytics to data science and on into the deep learning horizons.

Prioritizing User Experience in Messaging Systems

Jowanza Joseph

Resource efficiency is one reason to utilize a messaging system, but the user experience may ultimately be a more compelling one. The software systems we use and rely on to manage our finances, run our businesses, and ensure our health all benefit from user experience enhancements. These enhancements can come in several forms, but the most notable are improving the design to make interfaces more comfortable to navigate and doing more on behalf of the user. Programs that perform on the user's behalf quickly and accurately can take an everyday experience and turn it into something magical. Consider a bank account that saves money on your behalf by using your balance and other context to deposit money in your savings account. Over time you save money without ever feeling the pain of saving. Messaging systems are the backbone of systems like this one and enable rich user experiences.

Consider another example from banking. In many cases, borrowing money requires printing out your bank statements, pay stubs, tax statements, and more so the bank can get an understanding of your monthly expenses. Frequently, these documents are required to prequalify for a loan and are required again two months later to get the actual loan. While this sounds painful and superfluous in an era of technology, the bank has good reason to be as thorough and intrusive as possible to manage risk and comply with regulations.

To modernize this credit approval system, we need to think about the problem through a slightly different lens. Here's one approach: after a customer prequalifies, the software system connected to the user's financial institution will send notifications to the lending company for predetermined events. The lender is notified in real time if the potential borrower does anything that would jeopardize the loan closing. In real time, the lender can update based on the borrower's behavior how much they can borrow and have a clear understanding of the probability that the loan will close successfully. After the initial data collection from prequalification, a real-time pipeline of transactions and credit usage is sent to the lender, so there are no surprises.

When something goes wrong in the medical field, it can be much more devastating than losing money. Mistakes in the medical field can lead to permanent injury and death for a patient, disbarment for a medical provider, or a lawsuit for a hospital system.

Of all patient complaints, the most common was that patients felt frustrated by having to give their medical history more than once per visit. How might a real-time system help the hospital?

The software engineering department and health providers at a Utah hospital worked together to reimagine what the health history system could look like. When a patient arrived at the hospital, they would enter their information on a tablet. Once complete, the data would be saved to the system. Three minutes before the scheduled appointment time, the doctor would receive a notification to log on and check the patient's information. During that time, they would end their previous appointment and start reading through the new patient's chart. When the doctor arrived in the patient's room, they would know everything they needed to know to start a conversation with the patient about their care.

This system even provided benefits after the initial consultation, including enabling the doctor to send test orders directly to the lab and auto-populating patient data when the patient checked in at the lab.

While initially designed to prevent duplicate collection of medical histories, the system ended up having a far-reaching impact on the hospital system. Not only did the hospital system save money, but the patient experience improved dramatically.

Privacy Is Your Problem

Stephen Bailey, PhD

Data has been called "the new gold" for its ability to transform and automate business processes; it has also been called "the new uranium" for its ability to violate the human right to privacy on a massive scale. And just as nuclear engineers can effortlessly enumerate fundamental differences in gold and uranium, so too must data engineers learn to instinctively identify and separate dangerous data from the benign.

Take, for instance, the famous *link attack* that reidentified the medical records of several high-profile patients of Massachusetts General Hospital. In 1997, MGH released about 15,000 records in which names and patient IDs had been stripped from the database. Despite the precautions, Harvard researcher Latanya Sweeney was able to connect publicly available voter information to these anonymized medical records by joining them on three indirect identifiers: zip code, birthdate, and gender. This left Sweeney with only a handful of records to sift through to reidentify many individuals— most notably, the governor of Massachusetts patient records.

Twenty years later, every business is an MGH, and every person with internet access is a potential Latanya Sweeney. Yet we all want a world where data is handled responsibly, shared cautiously, and leveraged only for the right purposes. Our greatest limitation in realizing that world is not one of possibility but responsibility; it's not a question of "How?" but "Who?"

I believe data engineers must be the ones to take ownership of the problem and lead. Controlling the reidentifiability of records through a single dashboard is good analytics hygiene, but preserving privacy in the platform delivering the data is crucial. Managing privacy loss is a systemic problem demanding systemic solutions—and data engineers build the systems.

The mandate to protect privacy does not translate to a boring exercise in implementing business logic; it presents exciting new technical challenges. How can we quantify the degree of privacy protection we are providing? How can we rebuild data products—and guarantee they still function—after an individual requests that their data be deleted? How can we translate sprawling legal regulations into comprehensible data policies while satisfying data-hungry consumers?

We will need to formulate a new set of engineering best practices that extend beyond the familiar domains of security and system design. Determining what is best practice *requires* much practice, though. It is essential that engineering leaders push their teams to understand and address the pertinent issues: the strengths and weaknesses of data masking, anonymization techniques like k-anonymization and differential privacy, and emerging technologies such as federated learning. Ultimately, data engineers should know the practice of *privacy by design* as intuitively as they do the *principle of least privilege*.

The alternative, if history is any guide, is a world in which institutions publish "anonymized" data to the world, and clever people and organizations reconstruct and repurpose private data for their own ends. Managing privacy, far from being an abstract concept for just philosophers and lawyers, has become a concrete problem perfectly suited for data engineers. It's time they made it their own.

QA and All Its Sexiness

Sonia Mehta

Before moving into a new home, prospective homeowners will hire an inspector to assess any damage within the house. Much like house inspectors, as data engineers, it's on us to spot any glaring and not-so-glaring issues with our data before sending it to production.

Setting up a quality assurance (QA) program is simple, and the gains are totally worth it! In setting up a QA program, tests can be divided into two major buckets: practical and logical.

Practical tests aim to test for completeness of the data and accurate data types. These include the following:

- Checking for data coverage by inspecting dates or expected row counts
- Standardizing currency inputs (e.g., removing commas from metrics)
- Ensuring that required fields contain no null values
- Validating for consistent date, time zone, and casing formats
- Confirming that headers are applied to data and not within the data itself
- Deduping the dataset

Logical tests are for business and domain relevance. This is the fun part! Integral to this step is obtaining a macro business context and understanding the main questions looking to be answered. It's also helpful to understand how important accuracy is to the stakeholder. Is directional accuracy sufficient, or is complete accuracy required? (Oftentimes finance teams will say that total accuracy is required, whereas other teams may be looking for only directional differences.)

This step includes applying subject-matter knowledge to the tests. For example:

- Every user in a trial should have $0 in their purchases total.

- The attribution event counts only if it happened before the installation, not after.

- The two sample sizes in the experiment should be within 1% of each other.

- Free users will never have access to these parts of the app, and therefore no data.

- If a user is refunded, ensure that the amount is deducted from the date of the refund, not the date of purchase.

Here are some additional notes on the QA process:

- The test is an equation. Assert what you expect for the field and compare this to the actual value. Voilà!

- Tools can help automate these tests during the development process to ensure consistency, accuracy, and stability.

- Use a linter!

- It's OK to have code rules. For example, maybe you want all True/False columns to begin with an `is` prefix, like `is_<question for true/false>`.

- As more people enter the organization and small changes across many individuals multiply, a well-thought-out QA program will help mitigate breakage.

- If you have more than one source of truth for a metric, use this as a QA method to keep both metrics in check.

- As new types of data arrive, new tests are needed.

Know that tests will break—and that's totally normal! You will be able to fix some relatively fast while others may require a significant refactoring because they exposed a hole in the code, and that's OK too! You may also find some errors that are outside your scope, like user entry fields; in these cases it's best to create reports of the erroneous entries and share them with the team responsible to help rectify the problem.

While implementing rigorous QA standards does not make you immune from blunders, it does help decrease their frequency and improve overall data sentiment. When folks can focus on the information that the data is telling us, organizations can expect to see higher data literacy and innovation.

Seven Things Data Engineers Need to Watch Out for in ML Projects

Dr. Sandeep Uttamchandani

According to a recent estimate, 87% (*https://oreil.ly/Vebmz*) of machine learning (ML) projects fail![1] This chapter covers the top seven things I have seen go wrong in an ML project from a data-engineering standpoint. The list is sorted in descending order based on the number of times I have encountered the issue multiplied by the impact of the occurrence on the overall project:

1. *I thought this dataset attribute meant something else.* (*https://oreil.ly/2ex0a*) Prior to the big data era, data was curated before being added to the central data warehouse. This is known as schema-on-write. Today, the approach with data lakes is to first aggregate the data and then infer its meaning at the time of consumption. This is known as schema-on-read. As a data engineer, be wary of using datasets without proper documentation of attribute details or a clear data steward responsible for keeping the details updated!

2. *Five definitions exist for the same business metric—which should I use?* Derived data or metrics can have multiple sources of truth! For instance, I have seen even basic metrics such as Count of New Customers having multiple definitions across business units. As a data engineer, if a business metric is being used in the model, be sure to look for all the available definitions and their corresponding ETL implementations.

3. *Looks like the data source schema changed.* This one is extremely common in large distributed teams. Schema changes at the source database

---

1 This chapter is a subset of a broader list of "98 Things That Can Go Wrong in an ML Project."
(*https://oreil.ly/vlE7S*)

are typically not coordinated with downstream ETL processing teams. Changes can range from schema changes (breaking existing pipelines) to semantic changes that are extremely difficult to debug. Also, when business metrics change, the business definitions lack versioning, making the historic data inconsistent.

4. *The ETL pipeline logic for training and serving is identical—not really!* The typical reason for model performance skew during training and inference is discrepancies in the training and serving pipelines. While the logic may start off identical, fixes made in one pipeline may not be reflected in the other. Especially avoid scenarios in which training and serving pipelines are written in different languages.

5. *Slow poisoning of the models.* It is easier to detect 0–1 kind of errors with data pipelines. The problems that are the most difficult to debug are the ones in which a table is being updated intermittently or is joining to a table that hasn't been updated correctly. In such scenarios, the models will degrade gradually and adjust to the changes. The key is building appropriate circuit breakers (*https://oreil.ly/TJNN3*) to detect and prevent bad-quality data during ingestion.

6. *All the datasets managed by a given team have the same quality.* This is a classic mistake. Not all datasets from the same team may be reliable. Some might be updated and managed very closely, while others are irregularly updated or have poorly written ETL pipelines! Always develop validation rules for any input data used by the models.

7. *Systematic data issues are causing bias in the overall dataset.* If errors in the dataset are random, they are less harmful to model training. But a bug that results in a specific row or column being systematically missing can lead to a bias in the dataset. For instance, if device details of customer clicks are missing for Android users because of a bug, the dataset will be biased for iPhone user activity. Similarly, sudden distribution changes in the data are important to track.

To wrap up, I believe ML projects are a team sport involving data engineers, data scientists, statisticians, DataOps/MLOps engineers, and business domain experts. Each player needs to play their role in making the project successful.

Six Dimensions for Picking an Analytical Data Warehouse

Gleb Mezhanskiy

The data warehouse (DWH) plays a central role in the data ecosystem. It is also often the most expensive piece of data infrastructure to replace, so it's important to choose the right solution and one that can work well for at least seven years. Since analytics is used to power important business decisions, picking the wrong DWH is a sure way to create a costly bottleneck for your business.

In this chapter, I propose six dimensions for evaluating a data-warehousing solution for the following use cases:

- Ingesting and storing all analytical data
- Executing data transformations (the *T* of *ELT*)
- Serving data to consumers (powering dashboards and ad hoc analysis)

Scalability

Businesses that choose poorly scalable data warehouses pay an enormous tax on their productivity when their DWHs cannot grow anymore: queries get backlogged, users are blocked, and the company is forced to migrate to a better-scaling DWH. However, at the point you feel the pain, it's already too late: the migrations are slow (years), painful, and almost never complete.

Scalability for data warehouses means three things:

- You can increase storage easily, whenever needed, and at a constant (if not diminishing) unit price.

- You can scale computing resources to have as many data-processing jobs as you need running concurrently without slowing one another down, and to shorten the execution time of each job.

- You can scale storage and computing resources independently of each other, depending on where the bottleneck is.

Price Elasticity

Pricing of DWHs falls into two main categories:

- Resource-based (e.g., pay per node of a certain configuration)
- Usage-based (e.g., pay per gigabyte of data scanned or CPU time)

Given the natural variability of analytical workload volume due to working hours and ETL/ELT schedules, usage-based pricing tends to be more economical for the following reasons:

- It aligns vendor incentives to your best interest by forcing them to increase the efficiency (speed) of their software. In contrast, vendors charging you per node are incentivized to sell you more computing resources instead of improving their efficiency.

- Usage-based pricing provides a clear path to cost optimization: use less to pay less. Simple tactics such as eliminating redundant subqueries in ETL processes or adding filters to dashboards are immediately effective in reducing costs.

Interoperability

Simply put, you want a DWH that's easy to get data into and out of. By picking a solution that is supported by the major collection, integration, and BI vendors, you will save yourself a lot of headaches.

Querying and Transformation Features

While feature requirements depend greatly on the nature of the business, keep these two considerations in mind regarding the functionality of a DWH:

- Optimize for the average user. Given that the vast majority of DWH users today are not engineers by training, prioritize their experience over power features.

- Your primary DWH does not have to tackle every specialized use case, including machine learning or geospatial and time-series analysis. If the DWH is interoperable, you can always plug in specialized software for the job.

Speed

One of the common failure scenarios in data infrastructure planning is over-optimizing for speed. At a tera/petabyte scale, data warehousing is all about trade-offs. You can't get infinite scalability and subsecond query speeds at the same time. Speed matters in two primary aspects:

- During workload/query development that is done on smaller data volumes, jobs should complete fast and fail fast to avoid blocking human workflows.

- In production, "good enough" execution time is good enough as long as it is consistent and can be maintained as the data grows (see the point about scalability).

A TPC-DS benchmark by Fivetran shows that most mainstream (as of 2021) engines are roughly in the same ballpark in terms of performance.

Zero Maintenance

Modern data warehouses are complex distributed software that is nontrivial to deploy and run, let alone develop. If you are tempted to go with a new promising open source engine, make sure to account for full cost of ownership and carefully evaluate the use case and trade-offs. Picking a DWH solution that does not require any resources for you to manage allows you to focus on building your customer-facing product.

Small Files in a Big Data World

Adi Polak

No matter whether your data pipelines are handling real-time event-driven streams, near real-time data, or batch processing jobs, when you work with a massive amount of data made up of small files, you will face the small files nightmare.

What Are Small Files, and Why Are They a Problem?

A *small file* is significantly smaller than the storage block size. Yes, even with object stores such as Amazon S3 and Azure Blob, there is minimum block size. A significantly smaller file can result in wasted space on the disk, since storage is optimized by block size.

To understand why, let's first explore how reading and writing work. For read and write operations, there is a dedicated API call. For write requests, the storage writes three components:

- The data itself
- Metadata with descriptive properties for indexing and data management
- A globally unique identifier for identification in a distributed system

More objects stored means extra unique identifiers and extra I/O calls for creating, writing, and closing the metadata and data files.

To read the data stored, we use an API call to retrieve a specific object. The server checks for the object's unique identifier on the storage server-side and finds the actual address and disk to read from. A hierarchy of unique identifiers helps us navigate the exabyte object storage capabilities. The more unique identifiers (objects) there are, the longer the search will take. This will result in lower throughput due to search time and disk seeks required.

Furthermore, this translates into an overhead of milliseconds for each object store operation since the server translates each API into remote procedure calls (RPCs).

When the server reaches its limits or takes too much time to retrieve the data, your API call for reading or writing will receive an error code such as 503 (server busy) or 500 (operation timed out).

Dealing with those errors is excruciating with Amazon Athena, Azure Synapse, and Apache Spark tools since they abstract the storage calls for us.

Why Does It Happen?

Let's look at three general cases resulting in small files.

First, during the ingestion procedure, event streams originating from Internet of Things (IoT) devices, servers, or applications are translated into kilobyte-scale JSON files. Writing them to object storage without joining/bundling and compressing multiple files together will result in many small files.

Second, small files can result from parallelized Apache Spark jobs. With either batch- or stream-processing jobs, a new file gets written per write task; more Spark writing tasks means more files. Having too many parallel tasks for the size of the data can result in many small files. Data skew can have a similar effect: if most of the data is routed to one or a few writers, many writers are left with only small chunks of data to process and write, and each of these chunks gets written to a small file.

Third, over-partitioned Hive tables can result from collecting data in tables daily or hourly. As a general approach, if a Hive partition is smaller than ~256 MB, consider reviewing the partition design and tweaking the Hive merge file configurations by using `hive.merge.smallfiles.avgsize` and `hive.merge.size.per.task`.

Detect and Mitigate

To solve the problem of small files, first identify the root cause. Is it the ingestion procedure, or offline batch processing? Check out your Hive partition file sizes, Spark job writers in the History Server UI, and the actual files' sizes on ingestion.

If optimizing the ingestion procedure to generate bigger files won't solve the problem, look at the Spark repartition functionality (`repartition_by_range`) and coalesce functionality to assemble small files together. Spark

3.0 provides partitioning hints (*https://oreil.ly/Nhz8x*) to suggest a specific assembling strategy to the Spark SQL engine.

Conclusion

Be aware of small files when designing data pipelines. Try to avoid them, but know you can fix them too!

References

- Microsoft: "Scalability and Performance Targets for Blob Storage" (*https://oreil.ly/CspBa*)
- AWS: "Optimizing Amazon S3 Performance" (*https://oreil.ly/RECIM*)

Streaming Is Different from Batch

Dean Wampler, PhD

Many organizations have a range of sophisticated analytics using tools like Hadoop, SAS, and data warehouses. These batch processes have the disadvantage of a potentially long delay between the arrival of new data and the extraction of useful information from it, which can be a competitive disadvantage. So why not move these analytics to streaming services? Why not process new data immediately and minimize delays?

Several challenges make this transition hard. First, different tools may be required. Databases may have suboptimal read and write performance for continuous streams. Use a log-oriented system (*https://oreil.ly/VKiTZ*) as your data backplane, like Apache Kafka (*https://kafka.apache.org*) or Apache Pulsar, (*https://pulsar.apache.org*) to connect streaming services, sources, and sinks.

Familiar analysis concepts also require rethinking. For example, what does a SQL GROUP BY query mean in a streaming context, when data keeps coming and will never stop? While SQL might seem to be a poor fit for streaming, it has emerged as a popular tool for streaming logic once you add *windowing*, for example over event time. A GROUP BY over windows makes sense, because the window is finite. It also enables large batch jobs to be decomposed into the small, fast increments necessary for streaming.

Now you're ready to deploy, but streaming services are harder to keep healthy compared to batch jobs. For comparison, when you run a batch job to analyze everything that happened yesterday, it might run for a few hours. If it fails, you'll fix it and rerun it before the next day's batch job needs to run. During its run, it might encounter hardware and network outages, or it might see data spikes, but the chances are low. In contrast, a streaming service might run for weeks or months. It is much more likely to encounter significant traffic growth and spikes, and to suffer hardware or network outages. Ensuring reliable, scalable operation is both harder and more important, as you now expect this service to always be available, because new data never stops arriving.

The solution is to adopt the tools pioneered by the microservices community to keep long-running systems healthy, more resilient against failures, and easier to scale dynamically. In fact, now that we're processing data in small increments, many streaming services should be implemented as microservices using stream-oriented libraries like Akka Streams (*https://akka.io*) and Kafka Streams (*https://oreil.ly/uJzDY*), rather than always reaching for the "big" streaming tools like Apache Spark (*https://spark.apache.org*) and Apache Flink (*https://flink.apache.org*).

To summarize:

- Understand the volume per unit time of your data streams.
- Understand your latency budget.
- Use Apache Kafka, Apache Pulsar, or similar as your data backplane.
- Use Apache Spark or Apache Flink when you have either large volumes or complex analytics (e.g., SQL), or both.
- Use microservices with stream-processing libraries like Akka Streams or Kafka Streams for lower-latency requirements and lower-volume situations.

Tardy Data

Ariel Shaqed

When collecting time-based data, some data is born late, some achieves lateness, and some has lateness thrust upon it. That makes processing the "latest" data challenging. For instance:

- Trace data is usually indexed by start time. Data for an ongoing interval is born late and cannot be generated yet.

- Collection systems can work slower in the presence of failures or bursts, achieving lateness of generated data.

- Distributed collection systems can delay some data, thrusting lateness upon it.

Lateness occurs at all levels of a collection pipeline. Most collection pipelines are distributed, and late data arrives significantly out of order. Lateness is unavoidable; handling it robustly is essential.

At the same time, providing *repeatable* queries is desirable for some purposes, and adding late data can directly clash with it. For instance, *aggregation* must take late data into account.

Common strategies align by the way they store and query late data. Which to choose depends as much on business logic as it does on technical advantages.

Conceptually, the simplest strategy is to *update existing data* with late data. Each item of data, no matter how late, is inserted according to its timestamp. This can be done in a straightforward manner with many databases. It can be performed with simple data storage. But any scaling is hard; for example, new data files or partitions need to be generated for late data. There is no repeatability (very late data might have arrived between repetitions of the same query), and any stored aggregations must be augmented, reprocessed, or dropped. This method is mostly suited for smaller scales.

Bitemporal modeling lets us add repeatability. If we add a second serialized *storage arrival time* field to all data, every query for analytics or aggregation can filter times by timestamp and then by a storage arrival time that is known (by serialization) to be in the past. Aggregates include the upper storage arrival time in their metadata, allowing queries to use them by filtering for the data that arrived later.

Another option is to *ignore* late data. Set a fixed deadline interval. Any data that arrives before the deadline is released for access and any data arriving later than the deadline is dropped (preferably with some observability). This is a simple option to understand, implement, and scale. But for repeatability, it delays all data by the deadline interval, *even when all data arrives on time*. So, it is most directly useful if there is a relevant deadline value.

Combine ignoring late data with an effective arrival time by *layering multiple instances* of this strategy. Set a sequence of deadline intervals. Data goes into the first layer not beyond its deadline, giving a quantized arrival time. Equivalently, data collection keeps a sequence of buckets with increasing deadlines. When a deadline expires, its bucket is sealed and a new one is opened with the same deadline. Queries are for a particular time and use only buckets that were sealed at that time; the time is part of the query, ensuring repeatability.

Tech Should Take a Back Seat for Data Project Success

Andrew Stevenson

Cofounder and CTO, Lenses.io

Data has always been a constant in my career. From my early days as a C++ developer tthrough my switch to data engineering, my experience managing increasing velocities and volumes of data for use cases such as high-frequency trading has forced me to lean on cutting-edge open source technologies.

I was one of the fortunate ones. I worked with an elite set of handsomely paid developers, at the peak of the big data revolution. Cutting-edge as we were, managing the technology wasn't our biggest challenge. Our top challenge was understanding the business context and what to do with the technology. As a dev, I shouldn't be expected to configure complex infrastructure, build and operate pipelines, and also be an expert in credit market risk.

Time and again, I witnessed business analysts sidelined in favor of data engineers who spent all day battling open source technologies with little or no familiarity with the context of the data or the intended outcome. The technology-first focus often led to Resume++, where technologists were empowered and enamored with technology rather than focusing on business objectives.

The result was slow progress, project failures, and budget overruns. This especially hurt businesses during the 2008 crash, and we're seeing that impact again starting in 2020 with COVID-19.

The greatest success and innovation I've witnessed occurs when end users (business users, data analysts, data scientists) are given the correct tooling and the access to explore, process, and operate data themselves.

Modern data platforms are distributed, generally open source, and their tooling, if any, isn't enterprise-ready. Therefore, organizations must turn to hard-to-find and highly skilled engineers. Unfortunately, these engineers have a limited understanding of the data and the business context.

Some organizations with "elite" R&D teams develop self-service tools at a huge expense. For those without the elite resources, these technologies are much less accessible. This exacerbates the divide between the web-scale companies (such as Google, Spotify, Uber, and Amazon) and the rest of the industry.

Technology should be an enabler to deliver data products. To achieve this, best-of-breed technologies should be available in a data mesh type of architecture with a decoupled self-service and governance layer. This allows end users to apply DataOps practices to operate data and applications without infrastructure knowledge. Workloads should include data cataloging, role-based access control (RBAC) options, data masking, and the ability to create virtual workspaces that allow teams to explore, process, and move data through low-code applications.

Cloud providers have created "technology intensity" by offering managed solutions for Apache Kafka such as Amazon MSK, Azure HDInsight, and Kubernetes. So, the role of data engineers should shift away from building pipelines and operating data infrastructure, to focus on delivering self-service tooling that allows end users to operate data themselves and build "data intensity."

Ten Must-Ask Questions for Data-Engineering Projects

Haidar Hadi

Think of this as a checklist of the questions that you need to ask before giving an estimate of when you will deliver or when you will start design. And you *definitely* need to ask these questions before coding.

Question 1: What Are the Touch Points?

Identify all the data sources that the data pipeline will be leveraging. Also identify all the output locations/systems that will be using the data product your pipeline produces, along with systems that contain configurations, lookups, etc.

Question 2: What Are the Granularities?

For a given data source, do not assume (based on the sample dataset) the granularity it represents. A given dataset may represent a transaction, a company, a combination of both, or an aggregation based on a certain level of granularity. Ask about the level of granularity on both the input data source and the output data source. For example, ask the following:

- Does the data object represent data on the transaction level; the transaction level rolled up to monthly, quarterly, or annually; or in a moving window?

- Does the data object represent data on the customer level (either an individual or a group of customers)?

Question 3: What Are the Input and Output Schemas?

Ask for the schemas for the input data sources and the output data sources before you start coding. Provide a sample output based on the input schema and the requirements you are given.

Question 4: What Is the Algorithm?

Most of the dataset produced by the data-engineering team will be fed into an algorithm that will produce a calculation or prediction. Make sure you understand the input for such an algorithm and compare it with the output dataset that you are supposed to produce. At the end of the day, the output produced by your data pipeline must have all the input elements to the algorithm at all stages.

Question 5: Do You Need Backfill Data?

Many algorithms use heuristics to build better predictions. However, during development, data scientists may focus on a smaller dataset, but still expect the full history backfill during production. Such requirements have an impact on development efforts, delivery date, resources, and cost.

Question 6: When Is the Project Due Date?

In many cases, the project may have dependencies on other projects. Clarify the due date in reference to other dependencies.

Question 7: Why Was That Due Date Set?

Now that you have clarified the project due date, please clarify the rationale behind it, as it may lead to more projects. Agreeing to a project due date without understanding its impact on the following project may give a false impression that you will be delivering multiple projects.

Question 8: Which Hosting Environment?

Ask for clarification on where the data pipeline will be running. Is it going to be hosted internally or on the cloud? What cloud accounts, permissions to the datasets, and resources will you be using?

Question 9: What Is the SLA?

Are the datasets produced in real time? In batches? When are they supposed to be delivered to the customer?

Question 10: Who Will Be Taking Over This Project?

Many projects will be maintained by other people. Ask about their skill level and the kind of documentation they need to operate your data pipeline.

The Data Pipeline Is Not About Speed

Rustem Feyzkhanov

Data-processing pipelines used to be about speed. Now we live in a world of public cloud technologies, where any company can provide additional resources in a matter of seconds. This fact changes our perspective on the way data processing pipelines should be constructed.

In practice, we pay equally for using 10 servers for 1 minute and 1 server for 10 minutes. Because of that, the focus has shifted from optimizing execution time to optimizing scalability and parallelization. Let's imagine a perfect data-processing pipeline: 1,000 jobs get in, are processed in parallel on 1,000 nodes, and then the results are gathered. This would mean that on any scale, the speed of processing doesn't depend on the number of jobs and is always equal to that of one job.

And today this is possible with public cloud technologies like serverless computing that are becoming more and more popular. They provide a way to launch thousands of processing nodes in parallel. Serverless implementations like AWS Lambda, Microsoft Azure Functions, and Google Cloud Functions enable us to construct scalable data pipelines with little effort. You just need to define libraries and code, and you are good to go. Scalable orchestrators like AWS Step Functions and Azure Logic Apps allow executing hundreds or thousands of jobs in parallel. Services like AWS Batch allow you to easily start a big cluster of instances with low Spot prices, use it to process jobs at scale, and terminate the cluster.

In addition, more and more vendors are introducing containers as a service, meaning that after you define an entity (e.g., Docker), it will be deployed and executed in parallel and you will pay only for processing time. Scalability is becoming low-hanging fruit that allows us to decrease processing times from days to hours and from hours to minutes.

But once we achieve perfect horizontal scalability, should we focus on execution time? Yes, but for a different reason. In a world of perfect horizontal scalability, execution time doesn't influence the speed of processing the batch much, but it significantly influences the cost. Optimizing speed twice means optimizing cost twice, and that is the new motivation for optimization.

This way, a decision about optimization becomes a decision about cost, which has a very clear return on investment (ROI). Even more, designing an absolutely scalable data pipeline without taking optimization of algorithms into account at all can lead to an extremely high cost for the pipeline. That is one of the disadvantages of a system that doesn't have an economy of scale.

The emerging opportunity is to design data pipelines to optimize unit costs and enable scalability from the initial phases, allowing transparent communication between data engineers and other stakeholders such as project managers and data scientists.

The Dos and Don'ts of Data Engineering

Christopher Bergh

CEO and head chef at DataKitchen

Here are the things that I wish I had known when I started out in the data industry years ago.

Don't Be a Hero

Data analytics teams work long hours to compensate for the gap between performance and expectations. When a deliverable is met, the data analytics team are considered heroes. Everyone loves to get awards at the company meeting; however, heroism is a trap.

Heroes give up work/life balance. Yesterday's heroes are quickly forgotten when there is a new crisis or deliverable to meet. The long hours eventually lead to burnout, anxiety, and even depression. Heroism is difficult to sustain over a long period of time, and it ultimately just reinforces the false belief that the resources and methodologies in place are adequate.

Don't Rely on Hope

When a deadline must be met, it is tempting to quickly produce a solution with minimal testing, push it out to the users, and hope it does not break. This approach has inherent risks. Eventually, a deliverable will contain errors, upsetting users and harming the hard-won credibility of the data analytics team.

Many data professionals will recognize this situation. You work late on Friday night to get high-priority changes completed. After a heroic effort, you get it done and go home. Saturday morning you wake up, startled. "I forgot to check X. Did I just break the analytics?" You can either rush back to work and spend the weekend testing, or let it go and hope everything is OK. In this context, hope is not a strategy on which to bank your reputation. You may get away with it a few times, until you don't.

Don't Rely on Caution

When the team finally buys into testing, a common mistake is to slow everything down. The project manager gives each data analytics project a longer development and testing schedule. Effectively, this is a decision to deliver higher quality but fewer features to users. Do this, and the data analytics team risks being viewed as bureaucratic and inefficient. Soon the VPs will each have their own data analyst on staff, and they'll wonder exactly what it is that you do.

Do DataOps

For many years, I accepted these things as just part of the job of a data professional. Then I realized that no, it doesn't have to be that way. I found that the software and manufacturing industries had been struggling with these same issues for decades. When I applied their methodologies to data engineering, I found my team could decrease the analytics cycle time and virtually eliminate errors.

This new approach is called *DataOps*, and you can implement it alongside your existing toolchain:

- Automate the creation of development sandboxes with data for data scientists.
- Use containers and other tools that simplify reuse.
- Manage parallel development and align toolchains with environments and source control.
- Push new analytics into operations by using DevOps continuous deployment.
- Create automated impact reviews and test, test, test.
- Orchestrate the code deployment and data operations pipelines, including tests.
- Architect for rapid change and quick recovery from outages. Design for the cycle time that you want.

When tests validate data flowing through the pipeline and also ensure the quality of all new and updated analytics, the error rate declines until errors are basically eliminated. There's no more need for heroism because the data pipelines are much more robust. There's no need for hope because your tests prove that the data and analytics are working. Most importantly, trust is maintained because analytics work as expected, and when they don't, the data team is activated with automated alerts. You'll know before the users, and they'll thank you when you call to give them a heads-up.

The bottom line here is that methodology and tools matter more than heroism. Automate everything that can be automated, and focus your attention on the creativity that requires a human touch.

The End of ETL as We Know It

Paul Singman

If you're as sick of this three-letter term as I am, you'll be happy to know there is another way.

If you work in data in 2021, the acronym *ETL* is everywhere.

Ask certain people what they do, and their whole response will be "ETL." On LinkedIn, thousands of people have the title "ETL developer." It can be a noun, a verb, an adjective, and even a preposition. (Yes, a mouse can ETL a house.)

Standing for *extract, transform, load*, ETL refers to the general process of taking batches of data out of one database or application and loading them into another. Data teams are the masters of ETL, as they often have to stick their grubby fingers into the tools and databases of other teams—the software engineers, marketers, and operations folk—to prep a company's data for deeper, custom analyses.

The good news is that with a bit of foresight, data teams can remove most of the ETL onus from their plate entirely. How is this possible?

Replacing ETL with Intentional Data Transfer

The path forward is with *intentional transfer of data* (ITD). The need for ETL arises because no one builds their user database or content management system (CMS) with downstream analytics in mind. Instead of making the data team `select * from purchases_table where event_date > now() - 1hr` every hour, you can add logic in the application code that first processes events and emits them in a pub/sub model (see the following figure).

With no wasted effort, the data team can set up a subscriber process to receive these events and process them in real time (or store them durably in

S3 for later use). All it takes is one brave soul on the data team to muster the confidence to ask this of the core engineering squad.

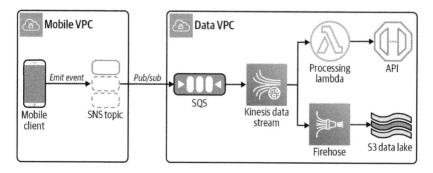

Ten years ago, data teams were beginning to establish their capabilities and needs, and such an ask might have been met with a healthy dose of resistance. A decade later, however, that excuse no longer flies. And if you are on a data team doing solely traditional ETL on internal datasets, it's time you upped your game.

There are several other benefits to IDT worth noting.

Agreeing on a Data Model Contract

How many times has one team changed a database table's schema, only to later learn the change broke a downstream analytics report? It is difficult to establish the cross-team communication necessary to avoid these issues when you have ETL scripts running directly against raw database tables.

With IDT, when an event occurs, it will be published with certain fields always present that are previously agreed upon and documented. And everyone knows that any change to this JSON contract needs to be communicated first.

Removing Data Processing Latencies

Most frequently, ETL jobs are run once per day, overnight. But I've also worked on projects where they've run incrementally every 5 minutes. It all depends on the requirements of the data consumers.

There will always be some latency between an event occurring and the data team receiving it, which introduces tricky edge cases to the data application.

With IDT, however, events are published immediately as they happen. Using real-time services like Amazon Simple Notification Service (SNS), Amazon

Simple Queue Service (SQS), and AWS Lambda, they can be responded to immediately.

Taking the First Steps

Moving from ETL to IDT isn't a transformation that will happen for all your datasets overnight. Taking one dataset to start, though, and setting up a pub/sub messaging pattern for it is extremely doable. My advice is to find a use case that will clearly benefit from real-time data processing—whether it's a feed of users' current locations or cancellation events—and then transition it from ETL to the IDT pattern.

The Haiku Approach to Writing Software

Mitch Seymour

Haiku is a traditional form of Japanese poetry that follows a specific set of rules. Haiku are designed to evoke deep emotion or understanding by using only three lines and a fixed number of syllables. For example:

> *First autumn morning*
> *the mirror I stare into*
> *shows my father's face.*
>
> —Murakami Kijo

As my experience as a software engineer grows, I have found myself writing better software by approaching it as I would a haiku. Here are some of the lessons I've learned along the way.

Understand the Constraints Up Front

When we build software, we must often operate within a narrow set of constraints. The constraints may include the business requirements, the technologies at our disposal, the skill set or bandwidth of the team, and the time we're given for actually creating the software.

Whether you're writing a haiku or software, if you ignore or don't understand the constraints of the project, you will have trouble producing what you set out to create. Instead of ignoring the constraints, aim to create something powerful or beautiful within them.

Start Strong Since Early Decisions Can Impact the Final Product

There's a lot of freedom in the initial stages of a project. Many engineers approach a new project in the way a painter might approach a blank canvas. They lay down some initial, wild brush strokes in the codebase with the intent to return later and add more structure or detail. This painterly approach doesn't always translate well, as the initial brush strokes often don't get layered upon at all, but are instead annotated with TODO-style comments and become permanent fixtures in the codebase.

The haiku approach is to be careful and intentional with early decisions, so that they become a strong foundation for everything that comes after. In other words, don't write the equivalent of the following haiku in your software:

> Something something // TODO
> the mirror I stare into
> shows my father's face.

Keep It as Simple as Possible

Unnecessary complexity can ruin a project. A haiku represents a body of work with all of the fat trimmed. Your codebase should be approached with the same care, as complexity threatens the long-term maintainability of your project and makes it easy for bugs to hide.

Simplicity is not always easy to achieve. In fact, it is often easier to write too much code than to find simpler, more efficient implementations. For the reasons I've stated, it's worth the extra effort to trim this extra fat from your codebase and keep it as succinct and simple as possible.

Engage the Creative Side of Your Brain

Writing software is an art form. It requires creativity, good decision making, and a lot of hard work. If you are uninterested in the project or the medium, it will be reflected in the final product. If you allow yourself to be challenged creatively, as a haiku writer would, you will be giving yourself an opportunity to create something impactful for your customers or business while having fun in the process.

The Hidden Cost of Data Input/Output

Lohit VijayaRenu

While data engineers are exposed to libraries and helper functions to read and write data, knowing certain details about the process of reading and writing operations helps you optimize your applications. Understanding and having the ability to configure various options can help with many data-intensive applications, especially at scale. The following are a few hidden details associated with data input/output (I/O).

Data Compression

While everyone agrees that compressed data can save disk space and reduce the cost of network transfer, you can choose from a plethora of compression algorithms for your data. You should always consider the compression speed versus compression ratio while choosing an algorithm. This applies to compression as well as decompression operations. For example, if the data is already heavy, choosing a faster decompression algorithm while sacrificing more resources for slower compression pays off.

Data Format

While most unstructured data is a collection of records, that might not be the best format for certain types of data access. For example, a record that has multiple nested fields, of which only a few are accessed frequently, is best stored in a columnar data format instead of a record format. You should consider using different levels of nesting versus flattening columns for efficient writing as well as data-retrieval operations. This also pays off in cost savings for your data storage.

Data Serialization

Most data is serialized into records using various formats. Structured data that is represented in various data formats should be serialized during writing and then deserialized every time it is read back. This process is usually hidden from users, but choosing efficient serialization/deserialization options (in a serde library) will greatly improve overall application performance at scale.

While there are many more aspects of I/O performance, knowing some of these details can help improve the overall performance of applications. Data engineers should take time to understand them and profile their applications to break down hidden costs associated with I/O.

The Holy War Between Proprietary and Open Source Is a Lie

Paige Roberts

Vertica Open Source Relations Manager

You don't have to choose sides in some imaginary holy war. Open source software can be great, so can proprietary software. The one metric to rule them all is: use what works best.

A lot of data engineers and architects feel like they have to pick a side between open source software and proprietary. You don't. Seriously, there are no sides.

The same engineers who write proprietary code often also write open source code. But which side of the line is open core software on? What about proprietary software with open source components, or proprietary software that allows you to embed or integrate open source components? Why the heck are you worrying about this? The only thing a data engineer should worry about is how to get a project into production most efficiently.

The main difference between an open source and a proprietary offering is that one was made by developers for developers, and the other was made by developers for customers. Customers tend to want greater ease of use and dependability. They'll settle for less control if it means they can get jobs into production faster, won't have to hire a specialist, and can rely on the solution. Developers want more power and control knobs. They'll settle for less ease of use and dependability if it means they get greater flexibility.

Power, flexibility, ease of use, speed to production, and dependability are all important. When you make your choice, think about the skills available to you, now and in the foreseeable future. Weigh the advantages of speed to production versus flexibility during the development stage. Think about the burden of ongoing maintenance, and your project's tolerance for occasional downtime. Consider whether any of those adjustment knobs are essential for your project.

Sometimes what works best will be open source software; other times, it will be proprietary. Sometimes building something from scratch is necessary, although that's likely to be the most expensive in time and expertise. Regardless of what you choose this time, nothing stops you from making an entirely different choice for the next job.

Also, consider integration. Best of breed makes a lot of sense, but if you spend half your time trying to get disparate software products to talk to each other, that isn't a win. Integration capability isn't an open source versus proprietary thing, either. Getting software built by one team to talk to software built by another is always a challenge. Even proprietary software from one vendor sometimes was built by multiple teams, and shoved together without much thought to making it integrate.

Choose software that works and plays well with others, particularly other software that you already know your project requires. And look at how much of the job a single application can accomplish. If one thing can do multiple parts of your task, that will reduce your integration burden.

Judge by your needs, your available resources, and what will give your project the best ROI.

The Implications of the CAP Theorem

Paul Doran

The CAP theorem (*https://oreil.ly/N0vRs*) forces us to compromise between consistency, availability, and partition tolerance in distributed data systems:

- *Consistency* means all clients see the same response to a query.
- *Availability* means every query from a client gets a response.
- *Partition tolerance* means the system works if the system loses messages.

As data engineers, we must accept that distributed data systems will have partitions, so we need to understand the compromise between consistency and availability. Constructing robust data pipelines requires us to understand what could go wrong. By definition, a data pipeline needs to move data from one place to another.

Here are three things to note about the CAP theorem's impact on system design:

- Attempting to classify data systems as being either CP or AP is futile. The classification could depend on the operation or the configuration. The system might not meet the theorem's definitions of consistency and availability.
- While the CAP theorem seems limiting in practice, it cuts off only a tiny part of the design space. It disallows those systems that have perfect availability and consistency in the presence of network partitions.
- The only fault considered is a network partition. We know from practice that we need to think about many more failure modes in real-world systems.

Having said that, the CAP theorem forces us to think about data system design. It forces us to ask questions about the systems we build and use. It forces us to ensure that we are meeting the needed requirements and expectations.

But the CAP theorem says nothing about what to do when things are running normally. The PACELC theorem (*https://oreil.ly/2tOL8*) builds on CAP and tells us that in the absence of partitions, the trade-off is between latency and consistency. If we are going to build and use highly available data systems, those systems will have to replicate data across nodes. A single node is a single point of failure.

This data replication is at the heart of the trade-off; how long are we willing to wait for data to replicate? We could wait for it to replicate to all nodes before making it available to ensure consistency, or we could keep the data available and accept that some users might see out-of-date data.

The data pipelines we build need to understand these choices. This is an important step toward building robust data pipelines. Extracting data from a database may require different choices than consuming data from a message queue.

The CAP theorem is an important result, but it is only a small part of the picture. It allows us to frame our thinking and understanding of the technologies we use, but it does not allow us to stop thinking about who our customers are and what they need.

The Importance of Data Lineage

Julien Le Dem

As a data engineer, you become a sort of *collector of datasets* coming from various sources. The challenge is that datasets don't just stay pinned on a board behind glass. They have to be maintained and updated in a timely manner. They have to be transformed and adapted to various use cases. They change form over time; all the layers built upon them have to be updated.

As data pipelines pile up, complexity increases dramatically, and it becomes harder to keep things updated reliably in a timely manner. Observing data lineage in all the layers of transformation—from ingestion to machine learning, business intelligence, and data processing in general—provides a critical source of visibility. With this information, the engineer on call can understand what's happening and resolve problems quickly when a crisis happens.

Lineage provides the understanding of how a dataset was derived from another one. *Operational lineage* goes one step beyond by tracing how and when that transformation happened. It captures information such as:

- The version of the input that was consumed
- The subset of the data that was read
- The version of the code doing the transformation
- The output's definition and how each column was derived from the input
- The time it took to complete and whether it was successful
- The version of the output that was produced
- The shape of the output data (schema, row count, distribution, ...)

Tracking operational lineage changes over time provides the critical information needed to quickly answer many questions arising when data-related problems occur:

My transformation is failing
> Did anything change upstream? Did the shape of the input data change? Where did this change originate? Did someone change the logic of the transformation producing it?

My dataset is late
> Where is the bottleneck upstream? How can this bottleneck be explained? Has it become slower recently? If yes, what has changed about its definition and its input?

My dataset is incorrect
> What changed in the shape of the data? Where upstream did the distribution of this column start drifting? What change in transformation logic is correlated with the change of data shape?

OpenLineage is the open source project standardizing lineage and metadata collection across the data ecosystem. With a data-collection platform in place, a data engineer can move fast and fix things fast. They can quickly perform impact analysis to prevent new changes from breaking things by answering such questions as: Will this schema change break downstream consumers? Who should be informed about this semantic change? Can we deprecate this dataset?

Lineage is also the basis of many other data-related needs:

Privacy
> Where is my users' private data consumed? Is it used according to user consent?

Discovery
> What datasets exist, and how are they consumed? How is this dataset derived from others? Who owns it?

Compliance
> Can I prove that my reporting is correctly derived from my input data?

Governance
> Am I using the data correctly?

As the number of datasets and jobs grows within an organization, these questions quickly become impossible to answer without collecting data-lineage metadata. This knowledge is the strong foundation that allows data to be manageable at scale.

The Many Meanings of Missingness

Emily Riederer

Missing data is possibly one of the best-explored topics in traditional data management; preventing null values is the textbook example for a database constraint, and detecting nulls is the same for data validation. However, missing data should not simply be dodged. By considering the many meanings of *missing*, data engineers can make more-thoughtful decisions about how to encode and communicate this missingness to end users.

It's tempting to think of missingness as a binary: the data exists or does not. However, this view ignores the potentially informative nature of nulls. *Missingness* can arise in numerous ways, each with its own analytical challenges. For example, a variable for an observation might appear to be missing because of the following:

- A true value for that variable exists, but it was loaded incorrectly.
- A true value for that variable exists, but it was intentionally uncollected.
- A true value for that variable exists, but it is unknown.
- No relevant value exists for that variable.
- The relevant value for that variable *is* null.

To illustrate, consider a dataset of users registering for an online ecommerce platform:

- A mismatch in account ID formats across tables, or arithmetic performed using a null and a non-null field, could introduce null values.
- A random sample of users is invited to complete a survey, and responses are recorded for only that sample.
- Users might be optionally asked for their birthdate. Every user *has* a birthdate, but only some are recorded.

- We might record whether mobile users registered from an Android or iPhone device, but there is no relevant value for users who registered from a Windows phone.

- Often retailers want to attribute user traffic to the referring source URL from which a user came. However, for users who type in the URL directly, the true value of the referring site is null.

For data analysts and scientists consuming your data, this distinction is more than semantics. Nulls that represent an issue loading data raise concerns about overall data quality; nulls from random sampling can possibly be safely ignored; nulls that represent aspects of user feedback could themselves become features in a model or analysis. (To continue one of the preceding examples, perhaps a user's unwillingness to share their birthdate could be a predictor of churn.)

As an engineer, you are closer to the generating system and may have more ability and insight to identify the root cause of missingness and pass this along. You can preserve far more information from the data-generating process by identifying the cause of missingness and thinking critically about how to represent this in the data. Should missingness be implicit (for example, no row in a table or field in JSON) or explicit? Should the value be null, a sentinel (e.g., a birthdate of 1900-01-01 or income of 999999999), or a shadow field (e.g., null in the main field with another field categorizing the missingness)? There's no one-size-fits-all solution, but recognizing and specifically designing for such nuance embeds value in an otherwise void of information.

The Six Words That Will Destroy Your Career

Bartosz Mikulski

Six words can destroy your credibility and jeopardize your career: "This number does not look correct." When you hear those words, it is already too late. People don't trust you anymore. They are suspicious about everything you have done so far. Suddenly, you become a person who makes mistakes—the person who has probably been feeding us false data for years.

Is there anything to worry about? What if the timing was terrible, and somebody recently made a wrong decision that caused the company to lose tons of money? Suddenly, every decision becomes data driven. Even the people who ignored the data for years claim that they were making data-driven decisions. The problem is that the data is incorrect.

The data is wrong because you have made a mistake! Congratulations! You've been promoted to a scapegoat! Everybody in the company is going to know your name. You have just become the Excuse of the Year.

Do you want that? No? What are you doing to avoid such a situation? How often are "hope" and "luck" a vital part of the data pipeline? We hope that the data format does not change. If we get lucky, the files get uploaded before we generate the report for the CEO. Of course, if it fails, we have a person who restarts it manually, and nobody notices the problem.

Data engineering is no different from other branches of software development. We can apply functional programming principles and turn our pipelines into something that resembles a function. Sure, the input is huge, and the function runs for a few hours, but for any given input, there is only one correct output, and we can write tests to ensure that we get what we expect. Does it seem trivial and obvious? So why are there so many data pipelines without a single line of test code?

The other best practices we can copy come from site reliability engineering (SRE) teams. These include relentless automation and monitoring. Manual configuration leads to systems that are fragile, unpredictable, and cannot be fixed. You never know what is going to happen when you change something. You can't create a test environment because you don't even know the current state of the production system. It's a nightmare.

Similarly, the lack of monitoring will make you wake up screaming at night. Do you know whether your pipeline processes all of the data? What if it drops 3% and nobody knows about it? We should gather instrumentation metrics about the code we run and about the data we process. You would be surprised by the number of issues you can detect by comparing the histograms of input values and the pipeline output.

Of course, all of that must be automated as a part of the pipeline, and the whole process must fail if any validation detects incorrect values. Otherwise, it becomes an expensive toy that nobody uses and nobody cares about.

The Three Invaluable Benefits of Open Source for Testing Data Quality

Tom Baeyens

As a software engineer turned data engineer, I can attest to the importance of data in organizations today. I can also attest to the fact that the software engineering principles of writing unit tests and monitoring applications should be applied to data. However, even though people know they should test data, they often don't have the good practices or knowledge to approach it. Enter open source. In this chapter, I explore three areas in which open source software presents data-testing benefits: for the data engineer, for the enterprise as a whole, and for the tools developers create and use.

Open source tools are developed by engineers, for engineers; if you're looking to start working with a data-testing tool that will naturally fit into your workflows, you have to start with open source. Open source software can also be embedded into data-engineering pipelines with ease: unencumbered by licensing restrictions or hidden costs, data engineers can be assured that open source tools will get to work quickly and easily.

For the enterprise, open source options have become a great way of getting started with data-quality initiatives. Implementing basic data testing and achieving better data quality in just a few days helps build the business case and starts uncovering data issues, helping avoid the pain of finding them too late. Open source projects allow for a frictionless approach to getting started and realizing results quickly. This enables far greater adoption by organizations and individuals. As a result, everyone can get closer to the data, and data teams can deliver high-quality, reliable insights with high velocity.

Combining open source software with a cloud-based platform gives everyone the tools they need, in the way they like them, to get to work. Data quality is a team sport, and combining open source with the cloud provides an integrated and collaborative approach that gives modern data teams what they need to create transparency and trust in the data. To me, best-practice open source is to allow a common library that supports everything from tool development to common enterprise solutions, all readily accessible to the entire organization.

And really, it's that ability to engage and innovate that gets to the heart of the biggest opportunity that open source software brings to data testing. They say it takes a village to raise a child, but the same could equally be said of creating good-quality data. Open source development is boosted in both speed and creativity through community engagement, coding, and testing. Whereas a commercial data-testing product may have a small team looking at it, open source projects benefit from whole communities of dedicated data analysts and engineers.

Open source software is opening up better data testing to those both within and outside the professional developer community. It's free, inclusive, built for purpose, and open to community-driven innovation—three invaluable benefits to improve data quality across all sectors.

The Three Rs of Data Engineering

Tobias Macey

In school we are told that the three Rs we need to know are reading, writing, and arithmetic. (I never did understand that, since only one of those words starts with R.) But once you grow up and get a job as a data engineer, you'll learn that there really are three Rs that you need to know, and in this case, they all actually start with that letter!

Reliability

At the end of the day, the most important characteristic of your data is that it needs to be reliable. All the fancy machine learning and sophisticated algorithms in the world won't do you any good if you are feeding them messy and inconsistent data. Rather than the healthy, beautiful, and valuable systems that you know they could be, they will grow up to be hideous monsters that will consume your time and ambition.

Reliability can mean a lot of things, but in this context we are talking about characteristics of your data that contribute to a high degree of confidence that the analyses you are performing can be assumed correct. Some of the elements of a data platform that is reliable are as follows:

- Consistent and validated schemas. All records follow the same pattern and can be treated the same way by your analytical processes.

- High availability of your systems to ensure read and write operations succeed. This requires systems that provide redundancy (there's another R word) in the face of server and network failures that are inevitable.

- A well-defined and well-maintained repository of metadata that will provide the necessary context around what the data is, where it came from, and how it was produced. These questions will get asked at some point, so it's best to have the answers ahead of time.

- Access control and auditability, to ensure that only the people and processes that are supposed to be able to modify the data are actually doing so.

Reproducibility

Reproducibility is a critical competency when working with business-critical systems. If there is no way for another team member or business unit to independently verify and re-create your datasets and analytics, there is no way to be certain that the original results were valid. This also factors into the concept of reliability, because if you are able to consistently reproduce a given dataset, you can be fairly sure that it is reliable and can be trusted to be available.

Repeatability

If all of your servers die, or the datacenter where your systems are running is destroyed or incapacitated by a natural disaster, you need a recovery plan. This is where the third R, *repeatability,* comes into play. It's all well and good to be able to build a Spark cluster or install a PostgreSQL database, but can you do it quickly and repeatedly? Having the configuration and procedures for repeating the installation or deployment of your data infrastructure feeds into the reproducibility of your data and the reliability of your analytics.

Conclusion

Now that you have learned the three Rs of data engineering, you can be confident that the teams and systems depending on the output of your labor will be happy and successful. Just be sure to let them know how much work went into it, so that they can fully appreciate your dedication and perseverance.

The Two Types of Data Engineering and Data Engineers

Jesse Anderson

There are two types of data engineering.[1] And there are two types of jobs with the title *data engineer*. This is especially confusing to organizations and individuals who are starting out learning about data engineering. This confusion leads to the failure of many teams' big data projects.

Types of Data Engineering

The first type of data engineering is *SQL-focused*. The work and primary storage of the data is in relational databases. All of the data processing is done with SQL or a SQL-based language. Sometimes this data processing is done with an ETL tool.

The second type of data engineering is *big data–focused*. The work and primary storage of the data is in big data technologies like Apache Hadoop, Cassandra, and HBase. All of the data processing is done in big data frameworks like MapReduce, Spark, and Flink. While SQL is used, the primary processing is done with programming languages like Java, Scala, and Python.

Types of Data Engineers

The two types of data engineers closely match the types of data engineering.

The first type of data engineer does their data processing with SQL. They may use an ETL tool. Sometimes their title is database administrator (DBA), SQL developer, or ETL developer. These engineers have little to no programming experience.

---

1 A version of this chapter was originally published at *jesse-anderson.com*.

The second type of data engineer is a software engineer who specializes in big data. They have extensive programming skills and can write SQL queries too. The major difference is that these data engineers have the programming and SQL skills to choose between the two.

Why These Differences Matter to You

It's crucial that managers know the differences between these two types of data-engineering teams. Sometimes organizations will have a SQL-focused data-engineering team attempt a big data project. These sorts of efforts are rarely successful (*http://www.jesse-anderson.com/2017/09/when-you-have-the-wrong-team-for-big-data/*). For big data projects, you need the second type of data engineer and a data-engineering team that is big data–focused.

For individuals, it's important to understand the required starting skills for big data. While there are SQL interfaces for big data, you need programming skills to get the data into a state that's queryable. For people who have never programmed before, this is a more difficult learning curve. I strongly recommend that SQL-focused people understand the amount of time it takes to learn how to program and the difficulty involved.

Only by knowing and understanding these two definitions can you be successful with big data projects. You absolutely have to have the right people for the job.

The Yin and Yang of Big Data Scalability

Paul Brebner

Chief technology evangelist, Instaclustr.com

Modern big data technologies such as Apache Cassandra and Apache Kafka achieve massive scalability by using clusters of many nodes (servers) to deliver *horizontal scalability*. Horizontal scaling works by sharing workloads across all the nodes in a cluster by *partitioning* the data so that each node has a subset of the data, enabling throughput to be increased by simply *adding more nodes*, and *replicating the data* on more than one node for reliability, availability, and durability.

Being intrinsically scalable, Cassandra and Kafka are popular open source choices to run low-latency, high-throughput, and high-data-volume applications, which can be easily scaled out. We recently designed, tested, and scaled a demonstration anomaly detection application with Cassandra for the storage layer, Kafka for the streaming layer, and Kubernetes for application scaling. The following figure shows the anomaly detection pipeline's application design, clusters, and "knobs."

Scaling is also hard! To get close to linear scalability with increasing nodes, we had to tune multiple software resources to enable the hardware resources to be efficiently utilized. The untuned system achieved 7 billion checks/day, but tuning resulted in a 2.5 times improvement.

The tuning "knobs" control hardware (cluster sizes) and software resources. By increasing the hardware resources (number of nodes in the Cassandra and Kafka clusters, and number of pods in the Kubernetes cluster), we were eventually able to scale to 19 billion anomaly checks per day. This was an arbitrary number to stop at; there is no theoretical upper limit. It was achieved with a total of 574 CPU cores (Kafka: 72 cores/9 nodes; Kubernetes: 118 cores/100+ pods; Cassandra: 384 cores/48 nodes). So, scaling is easy just by adding hardware resources, but this isn't the complete story.

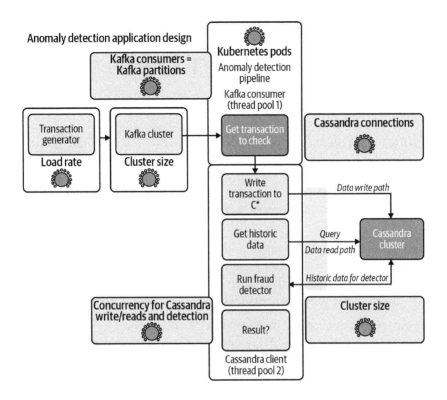

The most critical parameter was the number of *Kafka partitions*. In Kafka, partitions enable higher Kafka consumer concurrency, so we assumed that more was better. However, we found that increasing the number of partitions beyond a critical number *significantly* reduced the throughput of the Kafka cluster.

Subsequent benchmarking revealed that Kafka cluster throughput is maximized with a "sweet spot" number of partitions, and throughput drops significantly—due to replication overhead—with too many partitions. So, counterintuitively, a critical part of the scaling process was optimizing the application pipeline to *minimize* the number of Kafka consumers and partitions to achieve the goal of *maximum* throughput.

It's also important to make sure you have good data models for both Cassandra and Kafka. For Cassandra, use high-cardinality keys and bounded partitions. For Kafka, ensure that the key cardinality is much higher than the number of partitions (to prevent Knuth's parking problem), and don't start too many consumers at once (otherwise, you may get rebalancing storms).

Threading and Concurrency in Data Processing

Matthew Housley, PhD

In a typical modern environment, data flows through complex distributed systems at each stage of a data pipeline, and servers must reliably maintain numerous connections to their peers. The Amazon Kinesis outage in late 2020 illustrates the consequences of ignoring concurrency problems.

The outage, which occurred on November 25, took down a large swath of the internet. In this discussion, I'll assume that you've read Amazon's official report (*https://oreil.ly/b9ZdR*). The report uncovers several engineering blunders, but we will focus primarily on the limits of thread-based concurrency.

Operating System Threading

> *Each frontend server creates operating system threads for each of the other servers in the frontend fleet.*

In Linux and most other modern operating systems, *threads* are a mechanism for allowing a CPU to execute a number of concurrent tasks far exceeding the number of available CPU cores. A thread gets access to a CPU core during an allotted time; when time runs out, thread state is dumped to system memory, and the next thread is loaded into the core. Rapid cycling allows the operating system to maintain the illusion that all threads are running simultaneously. Threads provide an easy mechanism for managing many network connections.

Threading Overhead

The new capacity had caused all of the servers in the fleet to exceed the maximum number of threads allowed by an operating system configuration.

Threads are expensive. Each thread maintains its own stack, so thousands of connections consume substantial system memory. Switching threads is slow, consuming on the order of a few microseconds of core time, and a large number of threads can drive a high rate of context switching. Linux imposes a thread limit to prevent systems from grinding to a halt because of thread overhead.

Solving the C10K Problem

Fortunately, the engineering community overcame the concurrency limitations of threads years ago. Nginx—first released in 2004—was designed from the ground up to serve more than 10,000 simultaneous clients (C10K) by tasking each thread to manage many connections. The Go programming language builds software on concurrency primitives—goroutines—that are automatically multiplexed across a small number of threads optimized to available cores.

Scaling Is Not a Magic Bullet

Cloud native engineers have internalized the idea that scaling and concurrency can solve any problem; tech companies now routinely spin up clusters consisting of thousands of instances, and single servers can manage over 10 million connections. However, the Kinesis outage reminds us that scaling is viable only when built on sound underlying concurrency engineering.

Further Reading

- "Summary of the Amazon Kinesis Event in the Northern Virginia (US-East-1) Region" (*https://oreil.ly/Cqn2U*) by AWS
- "AWS Reveals It Broke Itself" (*https://oreil.ly/j6fM1*) by Simon Sharwood
- "Maximum Number of Threads per Process in Linux?" (*https://oreil.ly/B4Tky*) on Stack Overflow
- "Make Your Program Slower with Threads" (*https://oreil.ly/DV2qp*) by Marc Brooker
- "nginx" (*https://oreil.ly/osg5g*) by Andrew Alexeev

- "The Secret to 10 Million Concurrent Connections: The Kernel Is the Problem, Not the Solution" (*https://oreil.ly/fH4ty*) by Todd Hoff

Three Important Distributed Programming Concepts

Adi Polak

Many data engineers create pipelines for extract, transform, load (ETL) or extract, load, transform (ELT) operations. During a transform (T) task, you might be working with data that fits in one machine's memory. However, often the data will require you to use frameworks/solutions that leverage distributed parallel computation to achieve the desired goal. To support that, many researchers have developed models of distributed programming and computation embodied in known frameworks such as Apache Spark, Apache Cassandra, Apache Kafka, TensorFlow, and more. Let's look at the three most used distributed programming models for data analytics and distributed machine learning.

MapReduce Algorithm

MapReduce (https://oreil.ly/Zo0y0) is a distributed computation algorithm developed by Google in 2004. As developers, we specify a map function that processes a key/value pair to generate a set of intermediate key/value pairs, and a reduce function that merges all intermediate values associated with the same intermediate key. This approach is an extension of the split-apply-combine strategy for data analysis.

In practice, every task is split into multiple map and reduce functions. Data is distributed over multiple nodes/machines, and each chunk of data is processed on a node. A logic function is applied to the data on that node, and later the reduce operation combines data via the *shuffle mechanism*. In this process, the nodes redistribute the data based on the map function key's output.

Later, we can apply more logic to the combined data or go for another round of split-apply-combine if necessary. The open source solutions implementing these concepts are Apache Spark, Hadoop MapReduce, Apache Flink, and more.

Distributed Shared Memory Model

Shared memory models originated from operating systems like POSIX and Microsoft Windows, in which processes running on the same machine needed to communicate over a shared address space. *Distributed shared memory models* try to meet the same need. In a distributed environment, multiple nodes/users communicate over a network and need access to the same data from various machines.

Today, there is no one partitioned global address space. However, in-memory databases provide an answer to that need by adhering to multiple data-consistency levels. This allows a distributed programming operation on the data, where processes can write and read. Available open source solutions providing in-memory database capabilities are Redis (*https://redis.io*), Apache Ignite, Hazelcast In-Memory Data Grid (IMDG), and more.

Message Passing/Actors Model

Actors are threads/objects that encapsulate state and behavior. They communicate exclusively by asynchronously exchanging messages that are placed into the recipient's mailbox, and allow for the flow of communications/messages without locks and blocks. Building a distributed computation system on top of this model thus has the benefit of avoiding locks.

When picking open source solutions for this, check for message guarantees. Can you guarantee that messages will be delivered at most once? At least once? Exactly once? This will influence your system's operations. Open source solutions that implement messaging are Apache Kafka, Apache Pulsar, and more.

Conclusions

Now that you are familiar with these concepts, you can start to understand the bigger picture of data architectures and where each of these concepts comes into play.

Time (Semantics) Won't Wait

Marta Paes Moreira and
Fabian Hueske

Data pipelines are evolving from storing continuously arriving data and processing it as bounded batches, to streaming approaches that continuously ingest and process unbounded streams of data. Usually, the goal is to reduce the latency between the time when data is received and when it is processed.

An important difference between batch and stream processing is the notion of completeness. In batch processing, data is always considered complete (as defined by the input), but stream-processing applications need to reason about the completeness of their input when ingesting unbounded streams of data. For example, a common task is to compute aggregates for regular time intervals, like counting the number of click events per hour. When implementing such a stream-processing application, you need to decide when to start and stop counting (i.e., which count to increment for an event).

The most straightforward approach is to count events based on the system time of the machine that runs the computation. This approach is commonly called *processing time*. While it is easy to implement, it has a bunch of undesirable properties, including these:

- The results are nondeterministic and depend on several external factors, such as load of the processing machine, ingestion speed, and backpressure.
- Processing time does not consider events that arrive out of order, which is always the case in distributed environments.

An alternative to processing time is *event time*. With event time, each event has an attached timestamp. For our example of counting clicks per hour, each click event would have a timestamp specifying the time when the click happened, and the streaming application would use the timestamp of the event to decide which count to increment. Event time produces deterministic results and correctly handles out-of-order data.

A good illustration of the difference between processing time and event time is the sequence of *Star Wars* movies: the year each movie was released corresponds to the processing time, and the actual chronological order of the action in the plots to the event time.

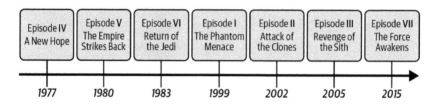

However, the challenge of reasoning about input completeness is not magically resolved by events with attached timestamps. An event-time application needs a mechanism to track its progress in time. Many stream processors, including Google Cloud Dataflow, Apache Beam, and Apache Flink, leverage watermarks for that.

A *watermark* is a metadata message that advances the time of the application. Operators use watermarks to decide up to which time computations can be performed. A cool property of watermarks is that they can be used to tweak the trade-off between latency and completeness. More-conservative watermarks lead to more-complete results with a higher latency, while tighter watermarks produce faster, yet possibly incomplete results.

In the end, there is no wrong or right in these semantic trade-offs for stream-processing applications. Just keep in mind that time really won't wait for your data. Unless you tell it to.

Tools Don't Matter, Patterns and Practices Do

Bas Geerdink

If you're taking a dive into the data-engineering world, it's easy to be overwhelmed by technical terms and frameworks. Most articles and books about big data start with extensive explanations about Apache Hadoop, Spark, and Kafka. Diving a bit further into the sister-realms of software development and data science, the list of programming languages and tools becomes a never-ending pile of strange-sounding terms, of which you tell yourself, "I should investigate this!"

I know plenty of engineers who keep track of lists of frameworks and tools that they have to dive into. However, that is not the way to go if you're just starting. Rather than learning the *tools* (frameworks, products, languages, engines), you should focus on the *concepts* (common patterns, best practices, techniques). If after studying you come across a new gimmick, doing some quick research should be enough to give you an idea of where to place it in the landscape.

But all these abstract concepts can also feel academic and high level. The key is to find learning resources with good examples. Search for books, blogs, and articles that don't jump straight to the source code, but explain general concepts and architectures.

When you come across an interesting piece of technology or a term that you're not familiar with, a trick is to always ask yourself the *why* question: Why must systems be distributed? Why is data governance needed? Why are there entire teams and products that are just doing ETL? Simply typing in these questions in a Google search or Quora will give excellent answers without the clutter of vendor/framework-specific details. After this, you can move to the *how* and *what*: How does this framework work? What use cases does it support? How does it interact with other technology? What are the costs of running this?

Here's some practical advice to help you on your way in the wonderful practice of data engineering. Pick a concept like data streaming, NoSQL, or functional programming that you're interested in, and do a quick internet search to learn the basics from documentation. Wikipedia is a great starting point. Then pick any tool that grabs your attention that is an example of the concept you're investigating (for example, Flink, Cassandra, or Scala). Block an afternoon for learning, spin up your terminal and favorite editor, and follow a set of tutorials. However, keep in mind when following along that you're learning a concept, and not the tool itself. Don't focus on details such as syntax and configuration too much, but rather keep asking yourself the *why* questions. Good luck!

Total Opportunity Cost of Ownership

Joe Reis

Choosing the right technology often comes down to cost—the time and money required. Total cost of ownership (TCO) is as ancient as enterprise software itself. While TCO has been a mainstay for decades, another cost is perhaps more onerous and far less discussed: total opportunity cost of ownership. As new technologies and paradigms come and go at an exponentially faster rate, companies need to keep their options open and take advantage of new and better ways of doing things.

TCO consists of two big areas: the asset's purchase price and the continued operating cost over the lifetime of that asset. Companies may choose to purchase managed solutions, implement and manage an open source solution, or roll their own. Each of these decisions has its own trade-offs for both the long and short term.

Apart from TCO, there are two aspects to choosing a technology: the technology itself and the paradigm it represents. You can invest in technology X, which is part of paradigm Y. For example, on-premises Hadoop (technology X) in the early 2010s was part of the new big data movement (paradigm Y). If you heavily invested in on-premises Hadoop in 2010, you probably felt like this was a smart move.

Fast-forward to 2020, and the terms "on-premises" and "Hadoop" both seem antiquated. Since 2010, the world has moved into the cloud, and there are many excellent alternatives to Hadoop. Meanwhile, your data team dedicates significant time and bandwidth to supporting the existing system. You likely have little time or energy to consider replatforming to a modern solution.

Total opportunity cost of ownership (TOCO) is the cost of being captive to technology X and paradigm Y, while no longer benefiting from new technologies and platforms. It's the price you pay by going all in on technology X and paradigm Y, and not being able to make the transition to new paradigms. Amazon founder Jeff Bezos urges people to opt for decisions with "two-way doors," meaning you can reverse course or take another direction. Lowering your TOCO allows you to move fast, experiment, and introduce new technologies and paradigms that can greatly improve your business.

Here are some suggestions to lower your TOCO:

- Avoid religious attachments to a particular technology or paradigm. Things change fast. As sure as the sun sets and rises, so will your favorite technology or paradigm eventually be obsolete.

- Separate computing and storage. Keep your data in object storage like Amazon S3, Azure Blob Storage, or Google Cloud Storage.

- Use containers. This allows portability of your code between platforms and clouds.

- Focus on core competencies and avoid undifferentiated heavy lifting. Invest in managed services whenever possible. Free up your time to invest in things that move the needle for your organization.

- Keep learning. Always be on the lookout for better ways of doing things.

Technology and paradigms change at light speed. Keep your options open.

Understanding the Ways Different Data Domains Solve Problems

Matthew Seal

Technology organizations commonly develop parallel tracks for multiple data concerns that need to operate in tandem. You often get a mix of teams that include data engineering, machine learning, and data infrastructure. However, these groups often have different design approaches, and struggle to understand the decisions and trade-offs made by their adjacent counterparts. For this reason, it's important for the teams to empathize with and understand the motives and pressures on one another to make for a successful data-driven company.

I have found that a few driving modes of thought determine many initial assumptions across these three groups in particular, and that knowing these motives helps support or refute decisions being made. For example, data science and machine learning teams often introduce complexity to tooling that they develop to solve their problems. Most of the time, getting a more accurate, precise, or specific answer requires adding more data or more complexity to an existing process. For these teams, adding complexity is therefore often a reasonable trade-off to value. Data scientists also tend to be in an exploratory mode for end results, and focusing on optimizing the steps to get there only slows that exploration when most things tried aren't kept anyway.

For data infrastructure, the opposite is often the desired path for success. Complex systems have lower reliability and require higher maintenance burdens to keep operational. Choosing building blocks that are optimized for the end goal is usually necessary to reliably reach scaling targets under cost. Additionally, data infrastructure teams are often tasked with scaling staffing sublinearly to the size of the data and business needs. The result of this combination is that infrastructure teams are always battling the cost of direct attention on existing systems and finding time to redesign the highest-criticality systems with patterns that can continue to grow ahead of the data intake. The stark contrast here between these first two groups' modus operandi can lead to heated conversations about the best ways to solve shared problems.

Finally, data engineers are usually tasked with precise and discrete tasks of producing tables of data. These usually have more well-defined outcomes and organizational requirements than their counterpart teams' problems. Tables need to be accurate, clean, and have a schema. Success depends on defining these contracts well for downstream consumers. Furthermore, they're usually under enormous time constraints to meet the demands of downstream teams. Thus, their solutions are usually focused on the immediate needs of a task and doing it as well as possible before moving on to the next. Designs for data-engineering workflows are usually aimed at solving a repeated task in a precise and efficient manner. Exactness and contracts are often more important than longer-term design for these problems. However, awareness of long-term problems is still a relevant and necessary concern that sometimes dictates designing a new pattern for a particular data problem before returning to the usual iteration cycle.

What's important to take from this is not that one group's focus is better than another's, but rather that if you're in one of these groups, you should be aware of your own design bias. The success criteria of our data efforts on a day-to-day basis will influence how we look at adjacent problems. Sometimes leaning on another way of thinking for solutions can lead to a design that better tackles upcoming concerns, but it's also valuable to recognize when a mismatched focus is being applied to a problem.

What Is a Data Engineer? Clue: We're Data Science Enablers

Lewis Gavin

The job title *data engineer* doesn't always come with the same sexy connotations as something like *data scientist*. Understandably, topics like machine learning and AI are always going to win the popularity contest. However, a good chunk of the work that sits behind these concepts stems from data engineering. I've seen a sea of articles recently talking about this exact point: that 80% of a data scientist's work is data preparation and cleansing.

AI and Machine Learning Models Require Data

Talk to any data scientist, and they'll tell you that obtaining data, especially from a source that has absolutely everything they require for their model, is a distant dream. This is where data engineers thrive.

The benefit of a data engineer is just that: the engineering. A data engineer can not only provide you with data from disparate sources, but also do it in a way that's repeatable, current, and even in real time.

Clean Data == Better Model

A 2016 survey (*https://oreil.ly/p63h7*) states that 80% of data science work is data prep and that 75% of data scientists find this to be the most boring aspect of the job.

Guess what—this is where the data engineer also thrives. They're great at joining, cleaning, manipulating, and aggregating data. All of this will be done in a repeatable way, providing a consistent source of fresh, clean data.

This allows data scientists to spend more of their time on improving the model, and their morale will be higher as the boring part of their job has now disappeared.

Finally Building a Model

The work of the data engineer doesn't stop here, as during the build, multiple iterations of the preceding steps will be cycled through. However, this section of the cycle is where the data scientist really shines, and I can't stress enough how important it is to let them do their thing here.

Everything I've talked about so far isn't me trying to say that data engineers are better or worth more. It's to show that they can enable more-efficient workflows for data scientists that let them get down to the nitty-gritty.

A Model Is Useful Only If Someone Will Use It

The model will need to be implemented in a real-world application, and if you're worried that the model will become stale in a few months, don't be. A good data engineer will be able to work with the data scientists and translate their work into something that can be fed new data, rebuild the model, and automatically deploy it.

So What Am I Getting At?

Data engineering is clearly an important field to consider. You can see just how much of the work behind building and deploying a data model can be accomplished by a data engineer.

The efficiencies gained mean that getting to the point of building the model will be quicker, and the resulting models will undoubtedly be better, as the data scientists have more time to spend tweaking and improving them.

What Is a Data Mesh, and How Not to Mesh It Up

Barr Moses and
Lior Gavish

We've seen how software engineering teams transitioned from monolithic applications to microservice architectures (*https://oreil.ly/pUdIJ*). The data mesh is, in many ways, the data platform version of microservices.

As first defined by Zhamak Dehghani, the original architect of the term, a data mesh (*https://oreil.ly/hIHce*) is a type of data-platform architecture that embraces the ubiquity of data in the enterprise by leveraging a domain-oriented, self-serve design. This idea borrows from Eric Evans's theory of domain-driven design (*https://oreil.ly/lhbFD*), a flexible, scalable software development paradigm that matches the structure and language of your code with its corresponding business domain.

Unlike traditional monolithic data infrastructures that handle the consumption, storage, transformation, and output of data in one central data lake, a data mesh supports distributed, domain-specific data consumers and views data as a product, with each domain handling its own data pipelines.

If you haven't already, we highly recommend reading Dehghani's groundbreaking article ""How to Move Beyond a Monolithic Data Lake to a Distributed Data Mesh" (*https://oreil.ly/ld0Mh*) or watching Max Schulte's tech talk on why Zalando transitioned to a data mesh (*https://oreil.ly/jLTU3*). You will not regret it.

Why Use a Data Mesh?

In 2021, the architecture du jour is a data lake with real-time data availability and stream processing, with the goal of ingesting, enriching, transforming, and serving data from a centralized data platform. For many organizations, this type of architecture falls short in a few ways:

- A central ETL pipeline gives teams less control over increasing volumes of data.

- As every company becomes a data company, different data use cases require different types of transformations, putting a heavy load on the central platform.

Such data lakes lead to disconnected data producers, impatient data consumers, and worst of all, a backlogged data team struggling to keep pace with the demands of the business.

Instead, domain-oriented data architectures, like data meshes, give teams the best of both worlds: a centralized database (or a distributed data lake) with domains (or business areas) responsible for handling their own pipelines.

The Final Link: Observability

The vast potential of using a data mesh architecture is simultaneously exciting and intimidating for many in the data industry. In fact, some of our customers worry that the unforeseen autonomy and democratization of a data mesh introduces new risks related to data discovery and health, as well as data management.

Given the relative novelty of data meshes, this is a fair concern, but we encourage inquiring minds to read the fine print. Instead of introducing these risks, a data mesh actually *mandates* scalable, self-serve observability (*https://oreil.ly/8wRDo*) in your data.

In fact, domains cannot truly *own* their data if they don't have observability. According to Zhamak, such self-serve capabilities inherent to any good data mesh include the following:

- Encryption for data at rest and in motion
- Data product versioning
- Data product schemas
- Data product discovery, catalog registration, and publishing
- Data governance and standardization
- Data production lineage
- Data product monitoring, alerting, and logging
- Data product quality metrics

When packaged together, these functionalities and standardizations provide a robust layer of visibility into your pipelines.

What Is Big Data?

Ami Levin

You've heard the term *big data* numerous times.[1] Articles and books have been written about it. You might be using a product that claims to be such. Perhaps you even have it on your resume. But have you ever stopped to think about what it really means?

Big data has no standard, clear, agreed-upon definition. Some use it to describe data volumes, others as an indicator of data velocity, or of data of a large variety. None of these have any quantitative metrics that can classify a dataset as being big or small. Many use it to refer to specific technologies such as Hadoop, while others use it to describe data from specific sources such as social media or IoT devices, or so called *unstructured* data.

So many conflicting, vague, and ambiguous definitions for big data exist, but none clearly describe the data or its use. Anyone can claim their products, services, technologies, or datasets to be "big data," and this claim can't be refuted.

The truth is that there is no such thing as big data. Large-volume, high-speed, varying-source data has always challenged our ability to derive value from it. Nothing fundamental has changed in the last decade to warrant a new term.

Data management has always been about applying analytical methods to gain insights that improve decision quality. Nothing more, nothing less. By now, you may be asking yourself why so many smart, honest, well-intentioned data practitioners believe that big data is a real thing.

Big data is nothing but a rebranding of existing offerings contrived by marketing people to revive interest and boost sales, and it is not the first time this has happened and probably won't be the last. In *Big Data at Work* (Harvard Business Review Press), Thomas Davenport says, "It is a well-established

---

1 This chapter was inspired by Stephen Few's book *Big Data, Big Dupe* (Analytics Press).

phenomenon that vendors and consultants will take any new hot term and apply it to their existing offerings—and that has already happened in spades with big data."

To find the root cause, all you need to do is follow the money trail. Big data advocates that you must store everything and keep it forever. It convinces organizations that they must use the latest technologies or they will be left behind. I'm sure you see where this is going.

Pursuing big data is a wild goose chase. It distracts organizations from what is really needed to uncover the value in data, encouraging them to invest in storage and the latest technologies instead of improving data quality and decision making—which can be achieved only with domain expertise, modeling skills, critical thinking, and communication. These require education, practice, and time. Unfortunately, those things are not as easy or sexy, nor as appealing, as the false promise of big data being the silver bullet that will solve all your data challenges.

We must refocus our efforts and stop chasing the latest fad, which is what we have been doing over and over again for decades. Reliance on any new technology, or a rebranding of an old one, is bound to fail. In my 25 years in data management, I have yet to see a technology that could beat a bad design.

What to Do When You Don't Get Any Credit

Jesse Anderson

Let's face it. Data engineers often don't get any credit. The praise rains down on the data scientists, but no credit rains down on the data engineering desert.

This isn't fair, and it's something I hear from data engineers consistently. Some are annoyed and disheartened by the lack of credit. Some are ready to quit because they see their careers going nowhere or fear they won't get a promotion.

Let's start with a few harsh realities. The CxOs, VPs, and other business people don't really care that you're using the latest technology, have unit tests, or have a scalable system in place. They care about the business value created by the data. (They only sort of care about these details when something goes wrong.)

You've probably heard that "data is the new gold." I agree with that statement. The issue is that data in and of itself is relatively worthless. Data becomes gold only after it is transformed into something that makes the business money or allows for a decision to be made.

If you think about the data value chain, the data engineering part usually doesn't create the business value—it facilitates the creation of business value. The data scientists and data analysts are the ones most commonly creating this business value. They're the ones who are front and center when some kind of analytic or insight is shown.

So, how do you start to get credit in your organization for what you do? As data engineers, we think that management should be interested in the technologies the organization is using. They aren't. That just isn't going to change.

Instead, we as data engineers need to start focusing on what the business people *are* interested in. We need to get in the habit of talking in language that they understand and care about. We need to explain that the analytics are possible only as a direct result of the data pipelines we've created.

We need to start tooting our own horns. Maybe the data scientists will even start tooting horns for us too. Start getting better at speaking the business language—and the credit, raises, and promotions will rain down upon you.

When Our Data Science Team Didn't Produce Value

Joel Nantais

I'm in my boss's office, briefing him on the new dashboard that will greatly increase access to data for everyone in the organization.

Like a slap in the face, he says, "Your data team can't get any meaningful data."

To say that this caught me off guard is an understatement. I knew the team was working hard. We had designed and launched several complex projects over the years.

Yet he didn't have confidence in our data or our ability to provide value.

Genuinely confused, I probed to learn more about his experience and perspective. He needed urgent, reactive responses to his data requests. Constantly, he heard we couldn't provide the data.

The priorities of the data team had focused on BI, ML, and forecasting tools. These were where the organization needed to be and had justified the increase in resources. Heck, we were following the five-year plan!

Looking back, I overfocused on the progress of our "sexy" long-term initiatives. And ad hoc data requests were not a priority. Only those requests with easy data access were fulfilled.

When you are in a reactive organization, you need to devote resources to that mission. I was determined to change the perception of our usefulness.

We worked to ensure that the team set a new culture of "getting to yes" no matter the effort. We reprioritized projects and held each other accountable.

Before this experience, we didn't have an exploration mindset. This was my fault. I had delegated specific tasks and requests without spending time to set expectations. I trusted my team members' expertise (correctly) but didn't explore the *why* for declined requests (incorrectly).

As a leader, it isn't enough to build the right team. You also have to form the right attitude and culture. You have to allow the needs of the organization to set the priorities.

How can you turn it around? If this sounds at all similar to the organization you work in, I recommend the following:

Five whys (https://oreil.ly/owM7t)
> This is my favorite tool. It allows you to push the team to understand true limitations.

Stakeholder engagement
> Spend significant time with requesters to understand needs. Engage a larger stakeholder group to get inconvenient data.

Domain knowledge
> Help the team lean on the subject-matter experts (SMEs), and make the discussions a two-way street. Show them your data, and have them walk you through their processes.

External awareness
> Get out of your office. Talk to the people in other offices. Understand their needs and wants.

In organizations that are not built around data science, you need to understand how your work contributes to the overall mission. When in a support role, have a genuine concern about the organization's needs and problems.

Understand how your tools can provide solutions. Balance long-term solutions with short-term needs. Usually, today's problem matters more than next year's problem.

When to Avoid the Naive Approach

Nimrod Parasol

They always say you should avoid overengineering. You just started the project and have no way of knowing what the future holds, so you should make the solution as simple as possible. Don't try to solve problems that do not exist yet. But sometimes the cost of postponing problems for later might be too high.

When you deal with large amounts of data, you find out that data migrations are complicated and costly processes. You need to write the code that transforms data from the old to the new format, then you need to run it over all your existing data, and eventually you need to perfectly synchronize the old and the new datasets in real time, so that consumers won't notice any change. This process is expensive in employee power and computer power and always carries the risk of introducing bugs into your production system.

When you design your data store, you should think about how to avoid data migrations in the future. There are two main factors to consider.

The first is the data storage *format*. It might be a database, or the file format you choose to use in your data lake. Once you decide on one, changing it will require either having a complicated system that supports both the old and new formats, or doing a data migration. Both are unwanted.

The second aspect to consider is the partition's *schema*. Most data stores today support schema evolution of some sort. You'll be able to add or remove fields fairly easily. But when you change the fields that partition the data, you have to migrate the data to the new partitions.

You might think that for starters, it'll be enough to use the company's default database technology without any partitioning. This might be true, but if you stop and consider these two points beforehand, you might notice optimizations that you already know you'll need to do in the future. So why not get rid of those right off the bat?

As with most things, there is no single universal truth. It might make sense to start with an un-optimized data store. Maybe it's still possible the project will never make it to production. Maybe you don't have any information about the expected query patterns, but need to quickly create a prototype.

When you do decide to go with the naive approach, you should know that if you let too much data accumulate before the optimizations, it will be expensive to do them later. In that case, it's best to mark milestones (either by data volume or business status) for revisiting the design before it becomes too late.

When to Be Cautious About Sharing Data

Thomas Nield

When I was fresh out of business school, I was taught that silos are bad and even toxic to organizations. When people and departments become too secluded and inwardly focused, all kinds of corporate dysfunction can happen. Redundant work becomes commonplace, contradicting and competing objectives undermine the efficacy of the organization, and valuable data that could benefit everyone stays locked away with its owners.

While these concerns are valid and do happen, I have learned that bureaucracy and silos sometimes exist for legitimate reasons. Data can become a political and organizational headache if it is made available to too many parties. "Why?" you ask in a surprised tone. "Shouldn't transparency and open data drive analysis and innovations?" Well, of course, but making data available is a balancing act and depends on the situation.

Let's get the obvious reasons that you should *not* share data out of the way first. If the data is sensitive, it is best to give access on only a need-to-know basis. If the database is vulnerable to heavy traffic and expensive analytical SQL queries, that is another obvious reason to not provide access. Typically, in that situation, you would provide a replicated database used for analysis, so it does not impact the production database.

Now I want to get into a less obvious reason: *sometimes domain experts should have exclusive access to a database and be its gatekeepers.* I know this sounds bureaucratic and terrible, and I too hate the phrase "leave it to the experts." But bear with me.

Sometimes navigating and interpreting specialized data correctly can be difficult, because doing so requires an immense amount of domain knowledge. If you know nothing about revenue forecasting, do you really have any business going through a revenue-forecasting database? Maybe you should ask the revenue-forecasting people directly for what you need! They know that data, the business it reflects, and which fields require a WHERE condition for your inquiry.

Say Joe works for a Fortune 500 company and transitions from one department to another. His new department asks if he can pull some strings to help get access to forecasting data from his previous department. Joe rightly tells them the implications of what they are asking for: the data is complicated and requires full-time expertise to interpret. It is not the type of database to browse casually, and it is easy to query incorrectly.

Not to mention, if Joe's new department starts doing his old department's work—well, that's going to complicate their organization, and this will perhaps step on some toes. When it comes to forecasting work, where should budget and talent be put now? Both departments? At best this may be a necessary organizational change, but at worst it can be a bitter and unnecessary political struggle.

Delegating responsibilities (and the data that goes with it) in an organization is no easy task. Centralizing data and making it accessible to as many stakeholders as possible is a noble objective, but it's not always practical. Some data should be shared more openly, while other data should be exclusively kept with its full-time experts who know it intimately enough to use it correctly.

When to Talk and When to Listen

Steven Finkelstein

As we approach the one-year anniversary on my current digitization project at work, I look back to see what can be learned from the experience. Project SWIFT was aimed at providing information about my employer's global manufacturing plants to the product developers earlier in the development process. The output would be a data-collection tool and a business intelligence report in Tableau. The objective was quite simple, but we encountered constant obstacles at the micro and macro level.

At the macro level, huge shifts were occurring in our organization. Our department was undergoing a strategic shift to the cloud and becoming more data driven. Significant organizational restructures happened, including the creation of a new data analytics team that absorbed my position. For new projects such as SWIFT, my team took the lead on the technical side, as opposed to IT in prior years. The organizational changes left a gap in leadership for critical design decisions. I believe this macro-level change was the foundation for the many challenges this project faced.

At the micro level, I was at the center of all requirements discussions. The data required for the final report did not exist, so early conversations were about what data needed to be captured, and the relationships between the entities being modeled. The initial request was translated into 35 data fields. Immediately, I pushed back against this request. We were employing an Agile methodology to get this project live as swiftly as possible. But as soon as we agreed on fewer fields, we hit a major obstacle.

The project added new subject-matter experts with more specialized knowledge. This resulted in previous requirements being questioned. Every ensuing meeting had 10 or more people attending. You had to be selective about which questions to ask and how to present the requests clearly. I remember constantly tweaking my approach to uncover which pairs of data fields had a many-to-many relationship. Sometimes my requests were interpreted incorrectly, but it was never entirely clear when I should enter a conversation. The best I could do was listen and wait for the right opening to correct the course.

As of today, we are still working on the project, but I am happy to say that we are live. While some ongoing challenges remain, we have made significant progress. The scope of the project was reduced to nine fields, and we designed the data model in third normal form to maximize flexibility for the business. Without the constant pushback from our team to reduce the complexity of the project, we would be nowhere near "go live."

This project provided many valuable lessons. Aiming for simplicity is essential in all discussions; however, understanding when it is our time to talk versus listen is extremely subjective. Steve Jobs said it best: "Our job is to figure out what they're going to want before they do." As a data engineer, sometimes you need to think like Steve Jobs in order to guide various stakeholders down the right path of technical simplicity, while still addressing their requirements.

Why Data Science Teams Need Generalists, Not Specialists

Eric Colson

In *The Wealth of Nations*, Adam Smith demonstrates how the division of labor is the chief source of productivity gains, using the vivid example of a pin factory assembly line: "One person draws out the wire, another straightens it, a third cuts it, a fourth points it, a fifth grinds it." With specialization oriented around function, each worker becomes highly skilled in a narrow task, leading to process efficiencies.

The allure of such efficiencies has led us to organize even our data science teams by specialty functions such as data engineers, machine learning engineers, research scientists, causal inference scientists, and so on. Specialists' work is coordinated by a product manager, with handoffs between the functions in a manner resembling the pin factory: "one person sources the data, another models it, a third implements it, a fourth measures it," and on and on.

The challenge with this approach is that data science products and services can rarely be designed up front. They need to be learned and developed via iteration. Yet, when development is distributed among multiple specialists, several forces can hamper iteration cycles. Coordination costs—the time spent communicating, discussing, and justifying each change—scale proportionally with the number of people involved.

Even with just a few specialists, the cost of coordinating their work can quickly exceed any benefit from their division of labor. Even more nefarious are the wait times that elapse between the units of work performed by the specialists. Schedules of specialists are difficult to align, so projects often sit idle, waiting for specialists' resources to become available. These two forces can impair iteration, which is critical to the development of data science products. Status updates like "waiting on ETL changes" or "waiting on ML

Eng for implementation" are common symptoms that you have overspecialized.

Instead of organizing data scientists by specialty function, give each end-to-end ownership for different business capabilities. For example, one data scientist can build a product-recommendation capability, a second can build a customer-prospecting capability, and so on. Each data scientist will then perform all the functions required to develop each capability, from model training to ETL to implementation to measurement.

Of course, these data scientist generalists have to perform their work sequentially rather than in parallel. However, doing the work typically takes just a fraction of the wait time required for separate specialist resources to become available. So, iteration and development time goes down. Learning and development are faster.

Many find this notion of full-stack data science generalists to be daunting. Particularly, it's the technical skills that most find so challenging to acquire, as many data scientists have not been trained as software engineers. However, much of the technical complexity can be abstracted away through a robust data platform. Data scientists can be shielded from the inner workings of containerization, distributed processing, and automatic failover. This allows the data scientists to focus more on the science side of things, learning and developing solutions through iteration.

With Great Data Comes Great Responsibility

Lohit VijayaRenu

The past decade has seen an explosion of data, affecting the way it is collected, processed, and analyzed at various organizations to better serve their customers. Many have embraced this change to become data-first companies. Both hardware and software systems have evolved to support big data systems, making it easy for data engineers to derive valuable insights that were never possible before. While data-driven applications have improved the user experience, user information can be exposed to applications and users beyond their control. Data engineers should now treat this information with greater responsibility.

Put Yourself in the User's Shoes

Multiple systems collect various kinds of personal information about users. Always handle users' information as you would your own. Data engineers should sometimes act as data guardians while designing data applications. We should always follow company or industry standards around security and privacy. An organization should have dedicated people or teams who help enforce security policies while making sure they are up-to-date against newer threats.

Ensure Ethical Use of User Information

Even with all the security policies enforced, it is the professional responsibility of data engineers to make sure user data is consumed in ethical ways. Advanced machine learning and artificial intelligence algorithms can easily predict user behavior and intent. We have to take time to think more about the implications of these algorithms and how they affect users' experiences and emotions.

Watch Your Data Footprint

As you build applications that consume data, you should also watch for how the output of your application is used. It is our responsibility to understand where and how the generated data is used, who has access to it, and what kinds of downstream applications are built using this data. This is also true if you are consuming data derived from other applications. Try to understand the intended usage and make an effort to expose its use to the original creator.

It is now more important than ever before for organizations to have a holistic view of how user information is used, what is derived from it, and who has access to this information.

Your Data Tests Failed! Now What?

Sam Bail, PhD

Congratulations—you've successfully implemented data testing in your pipeline! Whether that's using an off-the-shelf tool or home-cooked validation code, you've taken the crucial steps to ensuring high-quality data insights. But do you also have a plan for what happens when your tests actually fail? In this chapter, we'll talk through some key stages of responding to data test failures and critical questions to ask when developing a data-quality strategy for your team.

System Response

Automated system responses are the first line of response to a failed data test. This could be either doing nothing, isolating "bad" data and continuing the pipeline, or stopping the pipeline.

Logging and Alerting

Which errors need alerting and which ones can simply be logged for later use? Which medium (email, Slack, PagerDuty, etc.) do you choose for the alerts to make sure they get noticed? When are they sent (instantaneously, at the end of a pipeline run, or at a fixed time)? And finally, are the alerts clear enough for the responders to understand what happened and the severity of the incident?

Alert Response

Who will see and respond to those notifications? Is there an on-call rotation? What is the agreed-upon response time? And do all stakeholders know who owns the response?

Stakeholder Communication

You'll want to let data consumers know that "something is up with the data" before they notice. While investigating the issue, it is also helpful to keep an open line of communication with stakeholders to provide updates on the issue-resolution process.

Root Cause Identification

The key to identifying the root cause of data issues is to be methodical about the following:

- Identifying the exact issue that's actually happening
- Identifying the cause of the issue

I recommend not taking test failures at face value. For example, a test for null values in a column could fail because some rows have actual null values or because that column no longer exists. It makes sense to dig into the cause of an issue only after it's clear what that issue actually is!

Issue Resolution

We can organize the issues causing data test failures into the following categories:

- The data is actually correct, but the tests need to be adjusted. This can happen when there are unusual, but correct, outliers.
- The data is "broken" but can be fixed. For example, we might have incorrectly formatted phone numbers. In this case, we can make the respective changes in the upstream data, if we have access, or add logic in the pipeline code to handle these issues.
- The data is "broken" and can't be fixed. This may happen with missing values, or when we simply don't have access to the source data. In this case, we can choose to isolate the "broken" records and continue running the pipeline without them, or we might have to adjust our downstream use of the data to account for those issues.

Contributors

Adi Polak

Adi Polak is a senior software engineer and developer advocate in the Azure Engineering organization at Microsoft. Her work focuses on distributed systems, big data analysis, and machine learning pipelines. In her advocacy work, she brings her vast industry research and engineering experience to bear in educating and helping teams design, architect, and build cost-effective software and infrastructure solutions that emphasize scalability, team expertise, and business goals. When Adi isn't coding or thinking up new software architecture, you can find her hiking and camping in nature.

Three Important Distributed Programming Concepts, page 177
Small Files in a Big Data World, page 132

Amanda Tomlinson

Amanda Tomlinson made a career change into software development six years ago, and has been working in data engineering ever since. Her interest in product thinking and applying it to the data-engineering process led to a move to a full-time product role, and she is now the product owner for broadband service data for UK telecoms company BT. Amanda lives in Belfast with her husband Neil and children Sophia and Phoebe.

Listen to Your Users—but Not Too Much, page 94

Amelia Wong

Amelia Wong is the cofounder of Alluxio, Inc. Prior to Alluxio, she cofounded and managed a private foundation focused on advancing education and medical research. She is still involved in the nonprofit sector as a partner at Silicon Valley Social Venture Fund and as Board Director of her foundation. She was a JD candidate at UC Berkeley's School of Law, and has a BA from UC Berkeley.

Embracing Data Silos, page 62

Ami Levin

Ami Levin is an avid relational data model and SQL practitioner and educator. He is an active volunteer in the community and co-leads the Silicon Valley Data Platform User Group. He speaks often at various user groups and conferences, teaches, and produces instructional videos for some of the top learning platforms, including LinkedIn Learning, O'Reilly, and Pluralsight. Ami has published several whitepapers, articles, and books, including a Microsoft whitepaper and an AWS Aurora migration guide. In addition, Ami has extensive hands-on experience as a data architect, data modeler, database designer, and SQL developer. He has designed, reviewed, and optimized some of the world's largest, most challenging, mission-critical data environments. Ami holds a US patent for the invention of an autonomous database performance optimization technology.

What Is Big Data?, page 191

Andrew Stevenson

Andrew Stevenson is the chief technology officer and cofounder of Lenses.io, the company bringing DataOps to real-time data technologies such as Apache Kafka. He leads Lenses.io's world-class engineering team and technical strategy. With more than 20 years of experience with real-time data, Andrew has led and architected big data projects for banking, retail, and energy sector companies including Eneco, Barclays, ING, and IMC, and is a leading open source contributor.

Tech Should Take a Back Seat for Data Project Success, page 139

Anthony Burdi

Anthony Burdi has a wide variety of engineering experience in areas including data quality, edtech, vehicle safety, renewable energy, hybrid vehicles, and defense. He has a masters from Stanford and a BS from MIT, and has studied at the Recurse Center for computer science. Prior to joining Superconductive, Anthony has both been an individual contributor and led teams of varied disciplines, including one that launched the largest permanent-magnet direct-drive wind turbine in the world. At Superconductive he has helped build the core Great Expectations open source tool and worked with partners including Prefect and Dagster to build integrations.

Let the Robots Enforce the Rules, page 92

Ariel Shaqed (Scolnicov)

Ariel Shaqed (Scolnicov) is a software engineer at Treeverse. He builds novel tools like lakeFS, an open source project to provide data lakes with a novel transactional model. He started generating big data back when 2 GB was "big," and has since worked for companies small and large on everything from genomics to network tracing. When not with his partner and three boys or working, he sometimes runs.

Tardy Data, page 137

Atul Gupte

Atul Gupte is product manager on Facebook's Oculus Team. While at Uber, he served as a product manager on the company's Product Platform team. At Uber, he drove product decisions to ensure data science teams were able to achieve their full potential by providing access to foundational infrastructure and advanced software to power Uber's global business. He graduated from the University of Illinois at Urbana-Champaign with a BS in computer science.

How to Build Your Data Platform like a Product, page 81

Barr Moses

Barr Moses is CEO and cofounder of Monte Carlo, a data reliability company backed by Accel and other top Silicon Valley investors. Previously, she was VP of customer operations at Gainsight, a management consultant at Bain & Company, and served in the Israeli Air Force as commander of an intelligence data analyst unit. Barr graduated from Stanford with a BS in mathematical and computational science.

Observability for Data Engineers, page 112
How to Build Your Data Platform like a Product, page 81
What Is a Data Mesh, and How Not to Mesh It Up, page 189

Bartosz Mikulski

Bartosz Mikulski is a data engineer, trainer, conference speaker, and bloggerwith 10 years of experience developing data-intensive backend applications and data pipelines in a diverse set of industries. He has worked on software for network sniffers, phone call recording equipment, investment banks, a company in the travel industry, wiki hosting services, and supply chain risk management. Bartosz blogs about building trustworthy data pipelines, MLOps, and automated testing in data engineering.

The Six Words That Will Destroy Your Career, page 164

Bas Geerdink

Bas Geerdink works as a technology lead in the AI and big data domain. His academic background is in artificial intelligence and informatics. Bas has a background in software development, design, and architecture with a broad technical view from C++ to Prolog to Scala. He is an author and regular speaker at conferences and informal meetings, where he brings a mixture of business cases, architecture, and source code to his audiences in an enthusiastic way.

Tools Don't Matter, Patterns and Practices Do, page 181

Bill Franks

Bill Franks is the director of the Center for Statistics and Analytical Research at Kennesaw State University. He is the author of *Taming the Big Data Tidal Wave* (John Wiley & Sons), *The Analytics Revolution* (Wiley), and the editor of *97 Things About Ethics Everyone In Data Science Should Know* (*https://oreil.ly/yUN4H*) (O'Reilly). Bill is a sought-after speaker and frequent blogger. His work, including the role of chief analytics officer for Teradata (NYSE: TDC), has spanned clients in a variety of industries for companies ranging in size from Fortune 100 companies to small non-profit organizations. You can learn more at *www.bill-franks.com*.

Data Engineering from a Data Scientist's Perspective, page 38

Bin Fan

Bin Fan is the VP of open source at Alluxio Inc. Prior to joining Alluxio as a founding engineer, he worked for Google to build the next-generation storage infrastructure. Bin received his PhD in computer science from Carnegie Mellon University on the design and implementation of distributed systems.

Embracing Data Silos, page 62

Bob Haffner

Bob Haffner is a consultant specializing in data-engineering solutions. He has held multiple roles in a career that has spanned 20-plus years and various industries. Bob started Inventive Data Solutions in 2017 along with his wife, Anna. He has developed a variety of data-engineering projects, from traditional ETL to cloud-based serverless pipelines. Follow Bob on Twitter @bobhaffner.

Perfect Is the Enemy of Good, page 115

Boris Lublinsky

Boris Lublinsky is a seasoned enterprise architect and developer. He is an evangelist/architect in IBM Quantum computing research. Previously, he was a principal architect at Lightbend, where he actively participated in the development of Lightbend Cloudflow, an integrated system for streaming data applications with popular open source tools. Boris has written books for John Wiley & Sons and O'Reilly and contributed to several open source projects. He is a frequent conference speaker and tutorial teacher, and a co-organizer of several user groups in Chicago. Boris has a PhD in control systems from St. Petersburg Polytechnic University.

Defining and Managing Messages in Log-Centric Architectures, page 50

Chris Moradi

Chris Moradi is a full-stack data scientist who loves building easy-to-maintain data pipelines and services. He's worked on projects ranging from helping low-income high school students access college to identifying and fighting credit card fraud. In his current role at Stitch Fix, he's building the next generation of outfit creation and personalization algorithms.

Focus on Maintainability and Break Up Those ETL Tasks, page 68

Christian Heinzmann

Christian Heinzmann is a results-driven, pragmatic leader and technologist based in the Philadelphia area. His decades of experience range from nimble startups that need things yesterday to larger companies that need things to work at scale. He has a passion for taking complex systems and making them boring so the business can concentrate on business problems. He loves both the craft of software engineering and the insights that the modern data stack unlocks. When Chris isn't at a computer you can find him trying to perfect his sourdough bread.

How Data Pipelines Evolve, page 79

Christian Lauer

Christian Lauer is an IT project manager in the field of data and analytics. He would describe himself as a big data enthusiast who is based in Hamburg and Kiel. One of his biggest interests is data engineering, and many of his projects take place in that field.

Five Best Practices for Stable Data Processing, page 66

Christiano Anderson

Christiano Anderson (Twitter: @dump) is senior data engineer at SHARE NOW. Prior to SHARE NOW, Christiano worked as a big data and cloud consultant. He is passionate about data pipelines, cloud computing, Python, Scala, Spark, and infrastructure automation, and he is a frequent speaker at technical conferences around the world. As an open standards and free software advocate, Christiano has contributed to many projects and groups over 20 years.

Automate Your Infrastructure, page 9

Christopher Bergh

Christopher Bergh is the CEO and head chef at Data-Kitchen. Chris has more than 25 years of research, software engineering, data analytics, and executive management experience. At various points in his career, he has been a COO, CTO, VP, and director of engineering. Chris is a recognized expert on DataOps. He is the coauthor of *The DataOps Cookbook* and *The DataOps Manifesto*, and a speaker on DataOps at many industry conferences. Chris has an MS from Columbia University and a BS from the University of Wisconsin–Madison.

The Dos and Don'ts of Data Engineering, page 146

Dean Wampler

Dean Wampler (@deanwampler) is an expert in data engineering for scalable, streaming data systems and applications of machine learning and artificial intelligence (ML/AI). He is a principal software engineer at Domino Data Lab. Dean is the author of "What Is Ray? Distributed Computing Made Simple," *Fast Data Architectures for Streaming Applications* (*https://oreil.ly/M4hZt*), *Programming Scala* (*https://oreil.ly/cVXxa*), and other books and reports from O'Reilly.

Streaming Is Different from Batch, page 135

Denise Koessler Gosnell, PhD

Denise Gosnell loves working with data and, even more so, exploring its interconnectedness. As an author, engineer, and data enthusiast, she's pushed the boundaries of the graph industry for over a decade. Her PhD research coined the concept "social fingerprinting" by applying graph algorithms to predict user identity from telecommunication interactions. Since her graduate work, she has designed, implemented, and advised graph projects across all industry verticals around the world. When she isn't obsessing over graphs or data, you can find her outside, probably hiking up mountains.

A (Book) Case for Eventual Consistency, page 1

Dipti Borkar

Dipti Borkar is the cofounder and chief product officer at Ahana, the PrestoDB company. She has over 15 years experience in relational and nonrelational data and database technology. Prior to Ahana, Dipti was VP of product & marketing at Alluxio, and VP of product marketing at Kinetica and Couchbase. At Couchbase she held several leadership positions, including Head of Global Technical Sales and Head of Product Management. Earlier in her career Dipti managed development teams at IBM DB2, where she started her career as a database software engineer. Dipti holds an MS in computer science from UC San Diego and an MBA from the Haas School of Business at UC Berkeley.

Effective Data Engineering in the Cloud World, page 56

Dhruba Borthakur

Dhruba Borthakur is CTO and cofounder of Rockset, responsible for the company's technical direction. He was an engineer on the database team at Facebook, where he was the founding engineer of the RocksDB data store. Earlier at Yahoo, he was one of the founding engineers of the Hadoop Distributed File System. He was also a contributor to the open source Apache HBase project. Dhruba previously held various roles at Veritas Software, founded an ecommerce startup, Oreceipt.com, and contributed to Andrew File System (AFS) at IBM-Transarc Labs.

Know Your Latencies, page 88
Know the Value per Byte of Your Data, page 86

Einat Orr

Einat Orr is the CEO and cofounder of Treeverse, the company behind lakeFS, an open source project that empowers data lakes with ACID guarantees. She received her PhD in mathematics from Tel Aviv University, in the field of optimization in graph theory. Einat previously led several engineering organizations, most recently as CTO at SimilarWeb.

Mind the Gap: Your Data Lake Provides No ACID Guarantees, page 104

Elias Nema

Elias Nema is a data caretaker with more than 10 years of experience. Recently, he is leading data-intensive teams in the space of personalization and recommendations. He is captivated by using data to solve the problems of users, building an analytics-focused engineering culture, and experimentation to make better and faster decisions. Find him at *eliasnema.com* or on Twitter as @EliasNema.

Analytics as the Secret Glue for Microservice Architectures, page 7
Getting the "Structured" Back into SQL, page 74

Emily Riederer

Emily Riederer is a senior analytics manager at Capital One, where she leads a team to develop and sustain data products (including data marts, analytical tools, and dashboards) for business analysts and executives. She is particularly passionate about bringing open source tools and culture to industry and empowering communities of practice within organizations. Emily enjoys blogging about all things data at *emilyriederer.netlify.com*, speaking at meetups and conferences, and co-organizing the annual satRdays Chicago conference. She is also a contributing author to *The R Markdown Cookbook* (CRC Press) and the developer of the R packages `projmgr` and `convo`.

Eric Colson

Eric Colson is the chief algorithms officer emeritus at Stitch Fix, where he built the team of over 150 data scientists. In his emeritus role he takes on research projects, provides mentoring, and manages the tech brand. Formerly, Eric was the vice president of data science and engineering at Netflix. He also held relevant positions at Yahoo, Blue Martini, Proxicom, and Information Resources. He holds a BA in economics (SFSU), MS in information systems (GGU), and MS in management science and engineering (Stanford).

Fabian Hueske

Fabian Hueske is a committer and PMC member of Apache Flink. He is one of the original authors of the Stratosphere research system, from which Apache Flink was forked in 2014. Fabian is a cofounder of data Artisans (now Ververica), a Berlin-based company devoted to fostering Apache Flink and its community. He holds a PhD in computer science from TU Berlin and is a coauthor of the book *Stream Processing with Apache Flink* (*https://oreil.ly/9AD2s*) (O'Reilly).

Time (Semantics) Won't Wait, page 179

Gleb Mezhanskiy

Gleb Mezhanskiy is CEO and cofounder of Datafold, a data observability platform that helps companies unlock growth through a more effective and reliable use of their analytical data. As a founding member of data teams at Autodesk and Lyft and head of product at Phantom Auto, Gleb built some of the world's largest and most sophisticated data platforms and developed tooling to improve productivity and data quality in organizations with hundreds of data users.

Six Dimensions for Picking an Analytical Data Warehouse, page 129

Gunnar Morling

Gunnar Morling (@gunnarmorling) is a software engineer and open source enthusiast at heart. He is leading the Debezium project, a distributed platform for change data capture (CDC). He is a Java Champion, the spec lead for Bean Validation 2.0 (JSR 380), and has founded multiple open source projects, such as JfrUnit, Layrry, and MapStruct. Gunnar is an avid blogger (*morling.dev*) and has spoken at a wide range of conferences including QCon, Java One, Devoxx, JavaZone, and many others. He's based in Hamburg, Germany.

Friends Don't Let Friends Do Dual-Writes, page 70

Haidar Hadi

Haidar Hadi works as data engineer at Intuit building large-scale data systems to help small businesses with their finances. He has 20 years of experience building platforms, with the last 10 years focusing on large-scale data projects. He is an expert in analyzing historic patterns of events and decisions, and developing data products to predict future market trends and corporate performance. Haidar's passions are Scala, DynamoDB, TDD, building scalable high-performance systems, software architecture, and public speaking. He is an active member of the software community in Silicon Valley.

Ten Must-Ask Questions for Data-Engineering Projects, page 141

Ido Shlomo

Ido Shlomo (Git: idoshlomo, Twitter: @idoshlomo85) is a leader, practitioner, and international speaker in data science and MLOps in the Fintech space. With over 10 years of experience, he is currently head of BlueVine's DS team in the US and previously was a macro researcher at the Eitan Berglas economics department at Tel Aviv University. Ido specializes in building and scaling data teams that provide end-to-end AI/ML solutions for financial risk, fraud detection, and user life cycle management. His personal passion is figuring out novel NLP solutions for consuming complex unstructured data.

Cultivate Good Working Relationships with Data Consumers, page 32

James Densmore

James Densmore is the director of data infrastructure at HubSpot as well as the founder and principal consultant at Data Liftoff. He has more than 10 years of experience leading data teams and building data infrastructure at Wayfair, O'Reilly Media, HubSpot, and Degreed. James has a BS in computer science from Northeastern University and an MBA from Boston College.

Data Warehouses Are the Past, Present, and Future, page 48

Jeff Magnusson

Jeff Magnusson has been involved in the big data and data infrastructure space for over a decade. As an engineer and leader of teams at Netflix and Stitch Fix, he has advocated for and created democratized and self-service data environments that seek to maximize the impact that algorithms and data scientists can deliver within their organizations.

Data Engineering for Autonomy and Rapid Innovation, page 36

Jesse Anderson

Jesse Anderson is a data engineer, creative engineer and managing director of Big Data Institute. He mentors companies all over the world, ranging from startups to Fortune 100 companies, on big data. This includes projects using cutting-edge technologies like Apache Kafka, Apache Hadoop, and Apache Spark. He is widely regarded as an expert in the field and for his novel teaching practices. Jesse has been published by Apress, O'Reilly, and Pragmatic Programmers. He has also been covered in prestigious publications such as *The Wall Street Journal*, *Harvard Business Review*, CNN, BBC, NPR, *Engadget*, and *Wired*.

Data Engineering != Spark, page 34
The Two Types of Data Engineering and Data Engineers, page 170
What to Do When You Don't Get Any Credit, page 193

Joe Reis

Joe Reis is a "recovering data scientist" and business-minded data nerd who's worked in the data industry for 20 years, with responsibilities ranging from statistical modeling to forecasting, machine learning, data engineering, data architecture, and almost everything else in between. Joe is the CEO and cofounder of Ternary Data, a data engineering and architecture consulting firm based in Salt Lake City, Utah. In addition, he volunteers with several technology groups and teaches at the University of Utah. In his spare time, Joe likes to rock climb, produce electronic music, and take his kids on crazy adventures.

Total Opportunity Cost of Ownership, page 183

Joel Nantais

Joel Nantais is an executive leader in the federal government with more than 15 years of experience leading complex, multinational operations including integrating data science solutions to solve a myriad of policy and operational challenges. He is currently a doctoral candidate researching the application of advanced data science techniques in the public sector.

When Our Data Science Team Didn't Produce Value, page 195

John Salinas

John Salinas is a staff data engineer with USAA. He's been developing applications, websites, and tools since 2001. John has a degree in English communications and a masters in computer science. His experience includes building applications and web services, managing content management systems, and building real-time streaming systems. He currently spends his time thinking about data engineering in the cloud, helping teams be successful with data-engineering best practices, and helping with some of the toughest problems at work.

Moving from Software Engineering to Data Engineering, page 110

Jonathan Seidman

Jonathan Seidman has spent over a decade working in the enterprise data space as a software developer, solutions architect, community organizer, author, and speaker. Currently, Jonathan is a technical writer at Databricks. Previously, he worked at Cloudera as a software engineer and solutions architect. Before Cloudera, he was a lead engineer on the big data team at Orbitz. Jonathan is a cofounder of the Chicago Hadoop User Group and the Chicago Big Data Meetup, a frequent speaker at industry conferences, and coauthor of *Foundations for Architecting Data Solutions* (*https://oreil.ly/WlqtX*) and *Hadoop Application Architectures* (*https://oreil.ly/VRSKt*) (both O'Reilly).

Metadata ≥ Data, page 100

Jowanza Joseph

Jowanza Joseph is a staff software engineer at Finicity and leads the development of Finicity's open banking event mesh. Previous to Finicity, Jowanza worked on the streaming data platform at Pluralsight, working with Apache Kafka, Akka, and Kubernetes at scale. Earlier, he worked with Apache Pulsar, using it to build a fully managed messaging and stream processing platform, that processed billions of messages per day. With his passion for distributed systems and messaging systems, Jowanza writes about these topics on his blog. Over the years, he has given talks at Strange Loop, Abstractions, O'Reilly Strata Conference, the Open Source Summit, and the Lead Dev.

Prioritizing User Experience in Messaging Systems, page 121

Julien Le Dem

Julien Le Dem is the CTO and cofounder of Datakin. He co-created Apache Parquet and is involved in several open source projects including OpenLineage, Marquez (LFAI&Data), Apache Arrow, Apache Iceberg, and a few others. Previously, he was a senior principal at Wework; principal architect at Dremio; tech lead for Twitter's data processing tools, where he also obtained a two-character Twitter handle (@J_); and a principal engineer and tech lead working on content platforms at Yahoo, where he received his Hadoop initiation. His French accent makes his talks particularly attractive.

About the Storage Layer, page 5
The Importance of Data Lineage, page 160

Katharine Jarmul

Katharine Jarmul is head of product at Cape Privacy, an encrypted machine learning platform. She is a passionate and internationally recognized data scientist, programmer, and lecturer. Previously, she held numerous roles at large companies and startups in the US and Germany, implementing data processing and machine learning systems with a focus on reliability, testability, privacy, and security. Katharine is an author for O'Reilly and a frequent keynote speaker at international software and AI conferences.

Consensual, Privacy-Aware Data Collection, page 30
Data Quality for Data Engineers, page 42

Kirk Kirkconnell

Kirk Kirkconnell is an Amazon DynamoDB senior developer advocate at Amazon Web Services. He has more than 20 years of experience developing, administering, and architecting high-performance relational and NoSQL databases. Kirk is passionate about helping developers get up to speed quickly, including the creation of force-multiplier content. He has been a presenter at various database and industry conferences in his career and can be found on Twitter @NoSQLKnowHow. When he's not working, Kirk enjoys growing his own food, forest and farm conservation, hiking, photography, and doing certain activities that scare most people.

Learn to Use a NoSQL Database, but Not like an RDBMS, page 90

Valliappa (Lak) Lakshmanan

Lak Lakshmanan is the director for data analytics and AI solutions on Google Cloud. His team builds software solutions for business problems using Google Cloud's data analytics and machine learning products. He founded Google's Advanced Solutions Lab ML Immersion program and is the author of three O'Reilly books and several Coursera courses. Before Google, Lak was a director of data science at Climate Corporation and a research scientist at NOAA. Follow him on Twitter at @lak_gcp, read articles by him on Medium, and see more details at *www.vlakshman.com*.

Business Dashboards for Data Pipelines, page 21

Lewis Gavin

Lewis Gavin is a data architect who has been writing about skills within the data community for four years on his personal blog and Medium. While studying for his computer science degree, he worked for the Airbus Helicopter team in Munich enhancing simulator software for military helicopters. He then went on to work for Capgemini, where he helped the UK government move into the world of big data. He is currently using this experience to help transform the data landscape at *easyfundraising.org.uk*, an online charity cashback site, where he is helping to shape their data warehousing and reporting capability from the ground up.

What Is a Data Engineer? Clue: We're Data Science Enablers, page 187

Lior Gavish

Lior Gavish is CTO and cofounder of Monte Carlo, a data observability company backed by Accel and other top Silicon Valley investors. Prior to Monte Carlo, Lior cofounded cybersecurity startup Sookasa, which was acquired by Barracuda in 2016. At Barracuda, Lior was SVP of engineering, launching award-winning ML products for fraud prevention. Lior holds an MBA from Stanford and an MS in computer science from Tel Aviv University.

What Is a Data Mesh, and How Not to Mesh It Up, page 189

Lohit VijayaRenu

Lohit VijayaRenu is part of the data platform team at Twitter. He concentrates on projects around storage, compute, and log pipelines for scale both on premise and in the cloud. Lohit worked at several startups before joining Twitter. He has a masters degree in computer science from Stony Brook University.

The Hidden Cost of Data Input/Output, page 154
Metadata Services as a Core Component of the Data Platform, page 102
With Great Data Comes Great Responsibility, page 205

Marta Paes Moreira

 Marta Paes Moreira is a developer advocate at Ververica and a contributor to Apache Flink. After finding her mojo in open source, she is committed to making sense of data engineering through the eyes of those using its by-products. Marta holds a master's in biomedical engineering, where she developed a particular taste for multidimensional data visualization, and previously worked as a data warehouse engineer at Zalando and Accenture.

Time (Semantics) Won't Wait, page 179

Matthew Housley, PhD

 Matthew Housley is a data-engineering consultant and cloud specialist. After some early programming experience with Logo, Basic, and 6502 assembly, he completed a PhD in mathematics at the University of Utah. Matt then began working in data science, eventually specializing in cloud-based data engineering. He cofounded Ternary Data with Joe Reis, where he leverages his teaching experience to train future data engineers and advise teams on robust data architecture. Matt and Joe also pontificate on all things data on Monday Morning Data Chat.

Threading and Concurrency in Data Processing, page 174

Matthew Seal

 Matthew Seal is a cofounder and CTO of Noteable, a startup building upon his prior industry-leading work at Netflix. He began his career at OpenGov and helped build their data platform before quickly rising to lead architect. He then went on to Netflix, where he had an opportunity to work on a variety of cutting-edge technologies and architectures at massive scale. Matthew holds an MS from Stanford in ML/AI and is a thought leader in the Jupyter community. He's a core maintainer of many Jupyter and nteract projects, such as papermill and, more recently, testbook.

Understanding the Ways Different Data Domains Solve Problems, page 185

Meghan Kwartler

Meghan Kwartler has been an IT consultant since 2008. Her career has spanned manufacturing, marketing, logistics, and financial services, where she has installed software solutions and helped define business processes to improve efficiency. She frequently works at the intersection of technology implementation and senior leadership strategy. Meghan is based in the Boston area, is passionate about improving organizational behavior with complimentary software, and is the author of DataCamp's "Writing Functions and Stored Procedures in SQL Server" course. She is also the director of yoga programming at Well-Being Fitness, where she teaches yoga to people who have experienced traumatic brain injuries and develops programs to share the healing power of yoga for all.

Demystify the Source and Illuminate the Data Pipeline, page 52

Dr. Tianhui Michael Li

Michael Li is the founder and president of The Data Incubator, a data science training and placement firm. Michael bootstrapped the company and navigated it to a successful sale to the Pragmatic Institute. Previously, he headed monetization data science at Foursquare and has worked at Google, Andreessen Horowitz, JP Morgan, and DE Shaw. He is a regular contributor to *The Wall Street Journal, Tech Crunch, Wired, Fast Company, Harvard Business Review, MIT Sloan Management Review, Entrepreneur*, Venture Beat, TechTarget, and O'Reilly. Michael was a postdoc at Cornell Tech, a PhD at Princeton, and a Marshall Scholar at Cambridge.

Engineering Reproducible Data Science Projects, page 64

Mitch Seymour

Mitch Seymour is a writer, speaker, software engineer, and musician. He enjoys building real-time data systems and is the author of *Mastering Kafka Streams and ksqlDB* (*https://oreil.ly/oXTWz*) (O'Reilly). Outside of work, he enjoys spending time with his wife and daughters, running a canine-focused non-profit called Puplift, and helping companies improve their products and product marketing with his consulting firm, Waveshaper Consulting.

The Haiku Approach to Writing Software, page 152

Mukul Sood

Mukul Sood has a deep background in data and analytics, with over 15 years of experience leading transformation initiatives across industry verticals. He has a passion for redesigning and replatforming data warehouses, analytics for performance and scale, governance using data engineering, cloud services, machine learning, and DevOps. He also has a keen interest in soccer coaching junior league in his hometown, Jersey City, and loves to take the family hiking, biking, camping, and enjoying the outdoors.

Data Pipeline Design Patterns for Reusability and Extensibility, page 40

Nimrod Parasol

Nimrod Parasol is a senior software engineer at Google with more than 10 years of experience designing and implementing large-scale data solutions. He enjoys sharing knowledge on different platforms and advocates for the fact that there is no single generic solution for all data problems (so you'd better expand your arsenal!).

When to Avoid the Naive Approach, page 197

Paige Roberts

Paige Roberts (@RobertsPaige) has worked as an engineer, trainer, support technician, technical writer, marketer, product manager, and consultant in the last 24 years. She has built data-engineering pipelines and architectures, documented and tested open source analytics implementations, spun up Hadoop clusters, picked the brains of stars in data analytics, worked with different industries, and questioned a lot of assumptions. She's worked for companies like Data Junction, Pervasive, Bloor Group, Hortonworks, Syncsort, and Vertica. Now, she promotes understanding of Vertica, distributed data processing, open source, high -cale data engineering, and how the analytics revolution is changing the world.

The Holy War Between Proprietary and Open Source Is a Lie, page 156

Paul Brebner

Paul Brebner has gained extensive R&D experience in distributed systems, software architecture and engineering, software performance and scalability, grid and cloud computing, and data analytics and machine learning since learning to program on a VAX 11/780. Paul is the technology evangelist at Instaclustr. He has been learning new scalable technologies, solving realistic problems and building applications, and blogging about open source technologies such as Apache Cassandra, Spark, Zeppelin, Kafka, Elasticsearch, and Redis. He has worked at UNSW, several tech startups, CSIRO, UCL (UK), and NICTA. Paul has an MS (1st class) in computer science and a BS (computer science and philosophy majors).

The Yin and Yang of Big Data Scalability, page 172

Paul Doran

Paul Doran (@dorzey) is a technical lead with over 10 years experience, most recently focused on data engineering. He applies lean and agile principles to big data, analytics, and machine learning. Paul has a PhD in computer science from the University of Liverpool.

The Implications of the CAP Theorem, page 158

Paul Singman

Paul Singman is currently a developer advocate for the lakeFS project, after several years on the analytics team at Equinox Fitness. He enjoys contextualizing the latest data trends and technologies in blog posts and talks, instead of getting caught up in the hype surrounding specific tools. He's spoken at various conferences and meetups, including the Postgres Conference and AWS re:Invent. When not working you can find him running, playing golf, and sleeping.

The End of ETL as We Know It, page 149

Pedro Marcelino

Pedro Marcelino is a scientific researcher developing new machine learning architectures to solve problems in the field of transportation management systems with a focus on prediction models. He received his PhD with distinction and honor from Instituto Superior Técnico for his dissertation on "A New Approach to the Management of Transportation Infrastructure Maintenance Using Machine Learning."'" Pedro has published several articles on machine learning in scientific peer-reviewed journals, as well as on well-known websites such as Kaggle and Towards Data Science. In his free time, Pedro loves to read and write about human and machine learning.

Fundamental Knowledge, page 72

Dr. Shivanand Prabhoolall Guness

 Prabhoolall Guness has 20-odd years of experience as a software engineer and research scientist/academic. He is passionate about computer vision and machine learning. He has a PhD in electrical engineering from the University of Kent, UK. His current research involves assistive technology, human–computer interaction, and machine learning. His work's primary motivation is to tackle challenging problems (i.e., real-world issues) and develop solutions—including algorithms and software tools—to solve them. Prabhoolall is interested in topics such as security, the state of privacy considerations for assistive devices, and privacy issues linked to machine learning applications. He wants to make the interaction between humans and machines more natural and intuitive using vision (camera and sensors) and machine learning.

Low-Cost Sensors and the Quality of Data, page 96

Prukalpa Sankar

 Prukalpa Sankar is the cofounder of Atlan, a collaborative workspace for modern data teams (like GitHub for engineering teams) that has been recognized as a Gartner Cool Vendor in DataOps. Prukalpa previously founded SocialCops, a global data-for-good company (and World Economic Forum Technology Pioneer) behind landmark projects like India's National Data Platform and global SDG monitoring in partnership with the United Nations. Prukalpa has been recognized in the Forbes 30 Under 30, Fortune 40 under 40, and CNBC Top 10 Young Business Women lists, and is also a TED speaker.

Modern Metadata for the Modern Data Stack, page 106

Raghotham Murthy

 Raghotham Murthy has been scaling data infrastructure for over 20 years. At Facebook he built a multitenant and multi-datacenter analytics infrastructure scaling to 100PB of data, and he was named by *WIRED* as one of the data brains behind the rise of Facebook. He then led engineering at Bebop, an enterprise application platform acquired by Google. As an Entrepreneur in Residence at Social Capital he saw a widespread need for simplified data infrastructure that enables data teams to focus on generating insights from data instead of the data plumbing. He started Datacoral, a platform for declarative data pipelines, to solve this problem.

Be Intentional About the Batching Model in Your Data Pipelines, page 13
Change Data Capture, page 26

Rustem Feyzkhanov

 Rustem Feyzkhanov is a machine learning engineer at Instrumental, where he creates analytical models for the manufacturing industry, and an AWS Machine Learning Hero. Rustem is passionate about serverless infrastructure (and AI deployments on it) and is the author of the book *Serverless Deep Learning with TensorFlow and AWS Lambda* and the course *Practical Deep Learning on the Cloud* (both from Packt). Also, he is a main contributor to an open source repository for serverless packages and a repository for the deployment of serverless workflows with AWS Batch, AWS Fargate, and Amazon SageMaker.

The Data Pipeline Is Not About Speed, page 144

Sam Bail

 Sam Bail is a data professional with a passion for turning high-quality data into valuable insights. Sam holds a PhD in computer science focusing on knowledge representation, automated reasoning, and the semantic web. She has worked for several data-centric startups in recent years, gaining deep experience with real-world healthcare data and data-quality infrastructure.

Your Data Tests Failed! Now What?, page 207

Sandeep Uttamchandani

Sandeep Uttamchandani has over two decades of experience in building data products/platforms as well as leading the overall data + AI/ML charter. Currently, he is the chief data officer and VP of engineering at Unravel Data Systems, driving the mission of using AI for DataOps. Prior to this, he was at Intuit, leading the data platform, products, and analytics/ML initiatives for the $3B QuickBooks product portfolio. Sandeep is an O'Reilly book author, holds over 40 patents, and is a frequent speaker at data and AI/ML conferences. He holds a PhD from the University of Illinois at Urbana-Champaign.

Seven Things Data Engineers Need to Watch Out for in ML Projects, page 127

Scott Haines

Scott Haines is a senior principal engineer with a passion for distributed systems and event-based architectures. He is currently working at Twilio, where he has helped drive Apache Spark adoption and develop best practices for streaming pipelines as well as emerging data technologies. He helped build the Voice Insights infrastructure, which is the eyes and ears into the telecommunications service, and has played a critical role in the best practices of other emerging Insights/Analytics products. In his free time, Scott enjoys writing articles, speaking at conferences, teaching at meetups, and mentoring other engineers.

Pipe Dreams, page 117
Preventing the Data Lake Abyss, page 119

Sean Knapp

Sean Knapp is the founder and CEO of the data engineering company Ascend.io. Prior to Ascend.io, Sean was a cofounder, CTO, and chief product officer at Ooyala, where he oversaw product, engineering, and solutions. He also played key roles in scaling the company to 500+ employees, Ooyala's $410M acquisition, as well as Ooyala's subsequent acquisitions of Videoplaza and Nativ. Before founding Ooyala, Sean worked at Google, where he was the tech lead for the legendary web search frontend engineering team, helping that team increase Google's revenues by over $1B.

How to Prevent a Data Mutiny, page 84

Shweta Katre

Shweta Katre is a technology enthusiast who believes that the key to successful IT implementations is a symphony of process, data, and technology. Her experience spans business and process analysis, product evaluation, database design, and management. Prior to starting her career, Shweta received her bachelor's degree in electronics engineering. She has specialized certifications in data analytics and blockchain. An avid writer, she explores the latest tech on the block to build effective data science solutions by incorporating DataOps and ModelOps in deployment cycles for continuous improvement.

Caution: Data Science Projects Can Turn into the Emperor's New Clothes, page 23

Sonia Mehta

Sonia Mehta (@ohiosonia) has over a decade of experience in data analytics and data engineering. Over her career, she has spearheaded efforts to modernize data pipelines and analytical infrastructure to serve business needs. She is most passionate about getting data teams aligned to company goals and providing continual data feedback loops.

A/B and How to Be, page 3
QA and All Its Sexiness, page 125

Stephen Bailey, PhD

Stephen Bailey is currently the director of growth analytics at Immuta. He has played many data roles: scientist, engineer, analyst, janitor. Stephen has a passion for learning and sharing with others, especially those trying to break into the data field. He holds a PhD in cognitive neuroscience and relishes the moments when he gets to engage with others about the big picture.

Privacy Is Your Problem, page 123

Steven Finkelstein

Steven Finkelstein (@datageneralist) is an experienced data analytics professional with a passion for all things related to tech and investing. He is always looking for the next software or stock that piques his interest. In early 2020, Steven started *thedatageneralist.com*, where he publishes his thoughts on data analytics and finance, including the occasional pun. The alias "The Data Generalist" was inspired by his experiences across the entire analytics spectrum, from gathering requirements to engineering and statistical modeling. Outside of work, Steven enjoys intramural sports, live music, and spending a significant amount of time at the beach.

When to Talk and When to Listen, page 201

Thomas Nield

Thomas Nield is a research consultant as well as an instructor at the University of Southern California. He enjoys making technical content relatable and relevant to those unfamiliar with or intimidated by it. Thomas has written two books, *Getting Started with SQL* (*https://oreil.ly/QVh35*) (O'Reilly) and *Learning RxJava* (Packt). He regularly teaches classes on analytics, machine learning, and mathematical optimization and has written articles like "How It Feels to Learn Data Science in 2019" and "Is Deep Learning Already Hitting Its Limitations?" Valuing problem solving over problem finding, Thomas believes in using solutions that are practical, which are often unique in every industry.

Beware of Silver-Bullet Syndrome, page 17
Most Data Problems Are Not Big Data Problems, page 108
When to Be Cautious About Sharing Data, page 199

Tobias Macey

Tobias Macey hosts the *Data Engineering Podcast* and *Podcast.__init__*, where he discusses the tools, topics, and people that comprise the data engineering and Python communities, respectively. His experience across the domains of infrastructure, software, the cloud, and data engineering allows him to ask informed questions and bring useful context to the discussions. The ongoing focus of his career is to help educate people, through designing and building platforms that power online learning, consulting with companies and investors to understand the possibilities of emerging technologies, and leading teams of engineers to help them grow professionally.

Maintain Your Mechanical Sympathy, page 98
The Three Rs of Data Engineering, page 168

Tom Baeyens

Tom Baeyens cofounded Soda with Maarten Masschelein in 2018. Tom is the chief technology officer and oversees the company's product development, software architecture, and technology strategy. He is passionate about open source and committed to building a community where data engineers can succeed using the Soda Data Monitoring Platform. Tom is known for building several successful open source workflow communities. He is the inventor of the widely used open source projects jBPM® (part of JBoss®, which was acquired by Red Hat, Inc.) and Activiti® (now part of Alfresco Software, Inc.). He also cofounded Efektif, the cloud process automation company. Tom holds a master's degree in computer science from KU Leuven.

The Three Invaluable Benefits of Open Source for Testing Data Quality, page 166

Tom White

Tom White is an independent software engineer. His long-term professional interest centers around large-scale distributed storage and processing. He has been a software engineer for over 20 years and for the last decade has worked in distributed systems, as a developer, committer, and mentor on numerous projects in the Apache Hadoop big data ecosystem. Tom is the author of *Hadoop: The Definitive Guide* (*https://oreil.ly/NgQIf*) (O'Reilly). For the last six years he has focused entirely on big data infrastructure for genomics projects, including GATK, Scanpy, and most recently Sgkit. He lives in the Brecon Beacons in Wales with his family.

Automate Your Pipeline Tests, page 11

Vijay Kiran

Vijay Kiran is a principal software engineer skilled in big data engineering with a passion for Scala, Clojure, and Agile methodologies. He works at Soda Data as head of data engineering and is the product lead for Soda SQL, an open source tool for data testing and monitoring. Vijay lives in the Netherlands with his wife Neha and dog, Bowerick Wowbagger. He holds an executive MBA from the Rotterdam School of Management, Erasmus University.

Building a Career as a Data Engineer, page 19

Vinoth Chandar

Vinoth Chandar is the creator of the Apache Hudi project, and continues to serve as the project chair at the ASF. He was a principal engineer with Confluent, working across different event streaming systems like Apache Kafka, ksqlDB, and Connect. Vinoth founded the data team at Uber and led its design/architecture through the hyper-growth phases of the company, ultimately pioneering the next-generation data lake storage architecture. Today, Uber houses one of the largest transactional data lakes on the planet, serving over 150-PB of data stored in Apache Hudi. Vinoth has broad experience with various large-scale data systems, having also worked on the Oracle database server/GoldenGate team and the LinkedIn Voldemort project.

Embrace the Data Lake Architecture, page 59

Index

bias, systematic data issues and, 128
big data, 191-192
  metadata as, 107
  problems with defining, 191
  scalability issues, 172-173
  small file problems, 132-134
  SQL versus NoSQL, 108-109
  three types of technology, 34
big-data-focused engineering/engineers,
  170
Bonewald, Silona, 78
business (algorithmic) logic, 36
business capabilities, structuring data science team around, 204
business context, for data projects,
  139-140
business data, on dashboards, 21-22
business goals, data platform production
  and, 81
business metrics, ML project failures and,
  127
business rules, as checks on data quality,
  46
buy-in, from stakeholders, 82

C

C10K problem, 175
canonical data model, 50
CAP (consistency, availability, partition
  tolerance) theorem, 158-159
career building, 19-20
Cassandra, 172
caution, not relying on, 147
change data capture (CDC), 26-27, 71
change log, 26
checkpointing, 118
close of books, 14-16
cloud technologies
  benefits of combining with open
    source for data quality testing, 166

effect on data pipeline construction,
    144-145
  effective data engineering in cloud
    world, 56-58
  managed solutions for Apache Kafka,
    140
  minimizing use of in testing, 12
column names, as contracts, 28-29
commit log, distributed, 71
compiled libraries, 120
compression (see data compression)
computation component of data pipeline,
  34
concurrency, Amazon Kinesis outage and,
  174-176
consent metadata, 30
constraints, haiku/software parallels, 152
containers as a service, 144
context (see data context)
contracts, column names as, 28-29
controlled vocabulary, for naming fields,
  28
coordination costs, 203
copying data, 57
cost-per-byte, value-per-byte versus, 86
costs
  of data input/output, 154-155
  of data pipeline construction in cloud
    computing era, 145
  price elasticity of data warehouses, 130
creational patterns, 41
creativity, haiku/software parallels, 153
credit (recognition), for data engineering
  work, 193-194

D

DAG (directed acyclic graph), 40-41, 78
dashboards, 21-22
data
  data engineers as provider of, 187
  metadata versus, 100-101

design patterns for reusability/modu-
    larity/extensibility, 40-41
evolution with business growth, 79-80
execution time issues, 144-145
message queues, 117
ML project failures and, 128
need for business data on dashboards,
    21-22
setting foundations before writing code
    for, 52-53
visualization as part of frontend, 78
data platforms
    adapting to specific business applica-
        tions, 139
    building like a product, 81-83
    defined, 81
    elements contributing to reliability, 168
    metadata services as core component
        of, 102-103
data preparation, 187
data privacy, 123-124
data processing, best practices for, 66-67
data products
    avoiding data mutiny when producing,
        84-85
    data platform as, 81-83
    need for generalists on design team,
        203
    perfection as enemy of the good in
        delivery of, 115-116
data provenance, 31
data quality, 42-43
    benefits of open source for testing,
        166-167
    in data lake over long term, 119-120
    data platform production and, 83
    data validation and, 46-47
    how good data turns bad, 112
    low-cost sensors and, 96-97
    potential problems in ML projects,
        127-128

reliability and, 168
data science projects
    business context/technology divide in,
        139-140
    data engineers as data science enablers,
        187-188
    engineering reproducible projects,
        64-65
data science teams
    generalists on, 203-204
    and managements' perception of value,
        195-196
data scientists
    addition of complexity to tooling by,
        185
    and data communities, 54
    data engineering from perspective of,
        38-39
    when team failed to produce value,
        195-196
data security, 44-45
data serialization, hidden costs of, 154
data silos
    continued need for, 62-63
    valid reasons for having, 62, 199
data stack
    disaggregation in cloud world, 56
    modern metadata for modern data
        stack, 106-107
data stores
    avoiding dual-writes, 70-71
    designing, 197
data structure frameworks, 120
data systems, implications of CAP theo-
    rem for, 158-159
data testing
    benefits of open source for data quality
        testing, 166-167
    dealing with failure, 207-208
data time window (DTW) batching model,
    13

data validation, 46-47, 92-93
data value chain, 193
data warehouses (DWHs), 48-49, 129-131
data-engineering projects, ten must-ask
   questions for, 141-143
data-flow logic, 36, 37
database administration, 38
database-replication software, 66
DataOps
   and data product development, 140
   importance to data engineering, 147
   latent documentation and, 77
datasets
   ML project failures and, 127
   reproducibility, 169
data_timestamp, 13
Davenport, Thomas, 191
decorator patterns, 41
Dehghani, Zhamak, 189
design patterns, 41
DevOps, data observability and, 113
directed acyclic graph (DAG), 40-41, 78
disaggregation, 56
discoverability, metadata services and, 102
distributed commit log, 71
distributed computing, 177-178
distributed data systems, 158-159
distributed shared memory models, 178
division of labor, specialists and, 203
documentation
   for data pipelines, 53
   latent, 77-78
domain experts (subject matter experts)
   exclusive database access for, 199
   Project SWIFT and, 201
domain-driven design, 189
DTW (data time window) batching model,
   13
dual-writes, avoiding, 70-71
DWHs (data warehouses), 48-49, 129-131

E

ELT (extract, load, transform)
   best practices for, 66-67
   companies in middle of growth stage
      and, 79
   data warehouses and, 48
embedded collaboration, 107
encryption
   of sensitive data, 45
   of sensitive fields, 31
end users, input on data projects from, 139
ethics, in handling of user information,
   205-206
ETL (extract, transform, load)
   best practices for, 66-67
   data latency, 89
   end of, 149-151
   from data scientist's perspective, 38
   implementing reusable patterns in, 36
   maintainability and, 68-69
   replacing with ITD, 149-151
   scaling, 79-80
European Union (EU), 30
Evans, Eric, 189
event time, 179
eventual consistency, 1-2
execution time, 144
extensibility, design patterns for, 40-41

F

facade patterns, 41
failure
   data tests, 207-208
   experiments, 4
FAQ lists, 78
feedback, from stakeholders, 82
forecasting data, domain knowledge to
   interpret, 199
frontend, latent documentation for, 77-78
fundamental knowledge, 72-73
fundamentals, defined, 72

G

General Data Protection Regulation
    (GDPR), 30
generalists, on data science teams, 203-204
goals, data platform production and, 81
Google Protocol Buffers, 120
growth, long-term, 82

H

Hadoop, 56, 100, 183
haiku approach to writing software,
    152-153
hardware, mechanical sympathy and,
    98-99
Hariri, Hadi, 17
heroism, reasons to avoid, 146
hidden costs, of data input/output,
    154-155
Hive, 100, 133
hope, not relying on, 146
horizontal scalability, 172

I

infrastructure automation, 9-10
ingestion, automation of data validation
    and, 93
innovation, data engineering for, 36-37
integration, proprietary versus open
    source software, 157
intentional transfer of data (ITD), 149-151
interoperability, data warehouse, 130
inventory control, eventual consistency
    and, 1-2
issue resolution, 208
iteration, 203

J

Jobs, Steve, 202
joins, when writing SQL queries, 75
Jupyter notebooks, 64

K

Kafka (see Apache Kafka)
Kafka partitions, 173
key performance indicators (KPIs), 7
knowledge, growth of, 72-73
Kubernetes, 172

L

late data, 137-138
latencies
    knowing your, 88-89
    removing by replacing ETL with ITD,
        150
latent documentation, 77-78
legacy data, data lakes and, 119-120
libraries, compiled, 120
Lindy effect, 72
link attack, 123
Linux, threads in, 174
listening, talking versus, 201-202
log-centric architectures, messages in,
    50-51
logging, data test failure and, 207
logical tests, for QA, 125
long-term solutions, short-term needs ver-
    sus, 195-196

M

machine learning (ML) projects, 127-128
machine learning teams, 185
maintainability, ETL tasks and, 68-69
maintenance, data warehouses and, 131
MapReduce, 177
Massachusetts General Hospital (MGH),
    123
mechanical sympathy, 98-99
message passing, 117-118, 178
message queue as a service, 117
messages, defining/managing in log-
    centric architectures, 50-51
messaging component of data pipeline, 35

Q

QPS (queries per second), 89
quality assurance (QA), 125-126
queries
    data warehouse features, 130
    value per byte of data and, 86
    writing SQL queries in a structured
        manner, 74-76
queries per second (QPS), 89
query latency, 88
questions, for data-engineering projects,
    141-143

R

random number generators, 64
RDBMS (see relational databases)
real-time dashboards, 21-22
recognition, for data engineering work,
    193-194
recovery, repeatability and, 169
Redshift, 48
relational databases
    as best model for most data problems,
        108
    ETL operations and, 38
    as faulty model for using NoSQL data-
        base, 90-91
reliability, in data engineering context, 168
remote procedure calls (RPCs), 133
repeatability, 169
replication lag, 26
reproducibility
    in data engineering context, 169
    as goal of data science projects, 64-65
reproducible data science projects, engi-
    neering of, 64-65
return on investment (ROI), 145
reusability, design patterns for, 40-41
root cause identification, for data test fail-
    ure, 208
RPCs (remote procedure calls), 133

rules, automated enforcement of, 92-93
runtime performance, speed of innovation
    versus, 69

S

S3, object stores and, 57
scaling and scalability
    Amazon Kinesis outage and, 175
    big data and, 172-173
    data pipeline construction in cloud
        computing era, 144
    data warehouses and, 129
    ETL, 79-80
    single-stage pipeline limitations, 59
schema changes, 127
schema management, 103
schemas, for NoSQL databases, 90
security
    automating security tests, 45
    metadata services and, 102
    transaction security, 66
    user information and, 205-206
sensors, low-cost, 96-97
serialization, hidden costs of, 154
shared memory models, 178
sharing of data, 199-200
short-term needs, long-term solutions ver-
    sus, 195-196
shuffle mechanism, 177
silos (see data silos)
silver-bullet syndrome, 17
simplicity, in software writing, 153
site reliability engineering (SRE) teams,
    164
small files
    big data and, 132-134
    defined, 132
SMEs (see subject matter experts)
Smith, Adam, 203
software engineering
    haiku approach to, 152-153

Milton Keynes UK
Ingram Content Group UK Ltd.
UKHW021938141123
432575UK00005B/20